Essential
Denmark

by
JUDITH SAMSON

P9-CAL-427

PASSPORT BOOKS
a division of *NTC Publishing Group*
Lincolnwood, Illinois USA
708-679-5500

Published by Passport Books, a division of NTC Publishing Group, 4255
West Touhy Avenue, Lincolnwood (Chicago), Illinois 60646–1975 U.S.A.

The contents of this publication are believed correct at the time of printing.
Nevertheless, the publishers cannot accept responsibility for errors or
omissions, nor for changes in details given. We are always grateful to
readers who let us know of any errors or omissions they come across, and
future printings will be updated accordingly.

Published by Passport Books in conjunction with The Automobile Association
of Great Britain.

Written by Judith Samson
"Peace and Quiet" section by Paul Sterry

Library of Congress Catalog
Card Number 93–85609
ISBN 0–8442–8907–8

10 9 8 7 6 5 4 3 2 1

PRINTED IN TRENTO, ITALY

Front cover picture: Hans Andersen's Little Mermaid, Copenhagen

.The weather chart displayed on **page 100** of this book is calibrated in °C
and millimetres. For conversion to °F and inches simply use the following
formula:

$$25 \cdot 4\text{mm} = 1 \text{ inch} \qquad °F = 1 \cdot 8 \times °C + 32$$

Contents

This book employs a simple rating system to help choose which places to visit:

 'top ten'

◆◆◆ do not miss
◆◆ see if you can
◆ worth seeing if you have time

Introduction and Background

INTRODUCTION

Denmark may be one of Europe's smallest countries, but it has a surprising amount to offer. Neither too foreign nor too remote, it has a universal appeal, with its magnificent beaches, unspoilt islands, historic towns and lively culture.

Apart from the peninsula of Jutland, Denmark comprises over 400 islands, about 60 of them inhabited and four accessible with a car. Some of the islands are now linked by elegant and awe-inspiring bridges. The coastline is extensive and mostly sandy, providing a perfect family holiday destination, while those who prefer to escape from the crowds will find a huge range of houses for rent on quiet islands, including traditional wooden summer-houses.

Copenhagen's Little Mermaid, fixed in bronze

INTRODUCTION

Andersen's tale of 'The Emperor's New Clothes', illustrated by Arthur Rackham

It is a misconception that Denmark is totally flat, although its highest point is only 567 feet (173 metres). The inland scenery is a diverse mix of rolling hills, heather-clad moors and fertile farmland, dotted with windmills, white-washed churches, thatched farmhouses and sleepy villages. And the sea is rarely out of sight. The towns are compact and easy to explore; many have an historic centre which has been lovingly restored, and probably a museum proudly displaying local antiquities. Copenhagen and the bigger cities have excellent museums and galleries which compare with any in Western Europe, and many towns have summer music festivals. One hallmark of all things Danish is the uniformly high quality, and this applies equally to food and accommodation. Only the freshest ingredients, especially fish, are used to produce attractive and appetising dishes; cleanliness and comfort are assured wherever you choose to stay, whether a top hotel or campsite. Danish inns (*kros*), many of them historic, are well worth sampling. The Danes themselves are friendly and helpful and their gift for languages goes a long way towards making visitors feel at home in this charming country.

In the Danish alphabet, the following letters come after z: Æ, Ø, Å. In lists, Legoland, for example, precedes Læsø, and Århus comes at the end of the alphabet. Å is the same as AA, and should be used instead of it, but the city of Aalborg prefers to use AA.

BACKGROUND

Denmark today is a small peaceful country,
welcoming visitors to its shores. Yet a thousand
years ago its Viking people had a fearsome
reputation throughout much of northwest
Europe. The fact that Greenland and the
Faroes are still within the kingdom of Denmark,
although they now have Home Rule
Government, demonstrates a long and
complex history.

The First Settlers

As the glaciers retreated around 12000BC and
forests gradually replaced bare tundra, early
settlers cultivated the flat land surrounding the
entrance to the Baltic Sea. Finds from Stone
Age passage graves and finely wrought items
from Bronze Age burial mounds (1800–500BC)
are now exhibited in many Danish museums.
The best preserved Iron Age finds (500BC to
AD800) include the body of a man found in a
peatbog.

An early Dane,
preserved in the
peat near Århus

The early inhabitants of what is now Jutland
spent most of their time fighting each other and
exploring the neighbouring areas. Then in
around AD500 a tribe from Sweden, who called
themselves Danes, settled in Jutland. By AD800
the power of Charlemagne's Franks had
extended to north Germany, where the
population was converted to Christianity. An
early Danish king, Godfred, tried to repel
Frankish forces from the area he considered
was his own.

The Vikings

As a counter-offensive to Frankish advances,
the Danes and Norwegians, known as
Norsemen or Vikings, raided all the territory
they could, including Britain, in their fast,
cleverly designed vessels (see their boats in
the Viking Ship Museum in Roskilde). King
Harald Bluetooth (AD950–985) espoused
Christianity and a separate Danish church was
set up in 1104. Under his grandson, Knud
(Canute), England briefly became part of an
Anglo-Scandinavian kingdom.
Valdemar the Great (1154–82) and his
successors consolidated royal power and
continued to expand along the south and east

coasts of the Baltic and much of the North Sea; Valdemar II subjugated Norway, but early in the 13th century Denmark lost power and the Baltic was dominated by the Hanseatic League. During the 14th century, Danish kings sought by conquest or marriage to build a larger realm and there was civil war as nobles tried to gain more power. The country was divided up and the inhabitants of southwest Sweden (Skåne) chose to go over to Swedish rule. Valdemar IV reclaimed land which had been given to the nobles, drove back German forces and sold Estonia. But when he attacked Gotland (off Sweden), many alliances were formed against Denmark.

The Union of Kalmar

Valdemar's daughter was the remarkable Margrete, who struggled in a Europe battered by a worsening climate and the ravages of the Black Death to combine the Nordic peoples. She had married the King of Norway, and after the untimely death of her young son she inaugurated the Union of Kalmar (1397), under which Norway, Denmark and Sweden would share a monarch. Norway remained part of the Kingdom of Denmark until 1814, bringing with it the far-flung islands of the Shetlands, Iceland, Greenland and the Faroes. Margrete's successor, her nephew, Erik of Pomerania, tried to oust the counts of Holstein who had invaded Schleswig, but it was only when a Holstein count, Christian I from the German family (Oldenburgs) inherited the Danish throne in the mid-15th century that things began to improve for Denmark.

The Danes are noted for their fair skin and blue eyes

In the 16th century Denmark tried again to break the stranglehold of the Hanseatic League but this aim became less important as sea routes to India and the Americas opened up. The Reformation (1536) spread Lutheranism from Germany, bringing the downfall of the Catholic bishops whose property was confiscated by the Crown. When Christian IV ascended the throne in 1588, the country had fully recovered from the seven years war (1563–70) against Sweden. His energetic building programme has left a fine legacy of Renaissance architecture in Copenhagen.

Vor Frelsers Kirke

Years of Turmoil

Religious and political divisions culminated in
the Thirty Years' War (1618–48) which ravaged
much of central Europe. Sweden battled it out
with Denmark and regained most of its
provinces except Bornholm and Denmark's
remaining provinces in Norway.

In 1660 King Frederik III deprived the nobility
of their privileges and proclaimed himself
absolute monarch. He reorganised the
country's defences, but the wars with Sweden
continued intermittently until 1720.

Much of the 18th century was marked by social
advancements such as granting civil rights to
the peasants and allowing them to buy or rent
land, but although Denmark had acted ahead
of political developments such as the French
Revolution, it nevertheless became caught up
in the Napoleonic wars that followed. As a
result, Britain restricted the maritime freedom
of neutral nations, and as Denmark had signed
a treaty of armed neutrality with other Baltic
powers, the British sent an expedition, led by
Nelson in 1801, which forced Denmark to
withdraw. Six years later Copenhagen was
bombarded by another British fleet; Denmark
was forced to side with Napoleon who
threatened to invade Jutland. Sweden's reward
for joining the enemies of France was that
Norway should be ceded to Sweden – which it
was – under the Treaty of Kiel (1814).

Constitutional Change

In 1849 Denmark became a constitutional
monarchy when King Frederik VII handed over
most of his power to a two-chamber

The Golden Age

The 19th century was, for Denmark, dominated
by the rise of Prussia, but internally there was a
period of peace which allowed the arts to
thrive. The years 1810–48 were considered the
Golden Age of Danish art, when sculptor Bertel
Thorvaldsen, writer Hans Andersen, philospher
Søren Kirkegaard, educator N F S Grundtvig,
and numerous painters including Eckersberg
and Købke, thrived.

BACKGROUND

parliament, making the country a very democratic one for its time.

The struggles in the south of Jutland continued: Schleswig (which was Danish) did not trust the new constitution and asked to be united with Holstein, already in the German Confederation. Bismarck, the Prussian Prime Minister declared war and Denmark lost Schleswig in 1864 – a loss which was to last 56 years – but the population retained the Danish language.

By the end of the last century, several political parties had come into being and the ideas of revolutionary socialism began to percolate through society: trades unions were formed and industrialisation got under way, helped by the newly built railways. Danish farmers switched from grain to dairy products and bacon, and created cooperatives, helping pave the way to their political power.

The new royal family grew into the unpretentious monarchy which is so well known today. Elections in 1901 led to the first democratic government, and the old aristocratic Denmark faded in 1915 when the electoral privileges of the upper chamber of parliament were removed and women were given the vote. World War I found Denmark neutral – the Battle of Jutland was fought off the north Danish coast. As a result of a post-war plebiscite, the people of Schleswig voted to return to Denmark and Iceland became an independent sovereign state.

A generation later the country was not so fortunate: Denmark was invaded in 1940 by Hitler's forces, but a strong resistance movement arose which sabotaged factories and saved thousands of Jews.

Post-war Denmark

After the war, closer ties developed with other Scandinavian countries and Denmark was a founder member of EFTA. Today it belongs to the Nordic Council, NATO and the EC (which Greenland left in 1985).

Denmark has a popular monarchy, headed by Queen Margrethe II, who has been on the throne for 20 years. She is married to Prince Henrik, with sons Crown Prince Frederik and Prince Joachim. The current (1992)

On duty

Government is a non-socialist coalition of the Conservative People's Party together with the Liberal Party. A total of 16 parties fought the last election, but only eight gained seats in the 179-seat Folketing (Parliament).

Denmark, with a population of just over 5 million, is one of the most prosperous countries in the world, with a very high standard of living. The widespread provision of nursery schools means that a high proportion of families have two wage-earners.

A Fanø toddler in traditional bonnet

The country's most serious problems now are the large national debt and the high level of unemployment, currently around 10 per cent. To pay for its generous welfare services, taxation levels are high. Whatever the family income, all children receive an allowance. Pensions are paid to those aged 67 and over, but early retirement is possible.

Manufacturing industries account for about a third of Danish production, (food, beverages, metal products) with agriculture and fisheries accounting for only about six per cent. Not surprisingly, Denmark strongly supports the EC's new liberal trade policies. It cares keenly about the environment and was the first country in Europe to appoint a Ministry of the Environment, whose wide brief includes protecting nature, controlling pollution and the preservation of ancient buildings.

Tourists will be impressed by the cleanliness of the towns and though many older cities were ravaged by fire their few surviving wooden buildings are often beautifully restored. Almost every town has the same layout: an industrial area on the outskirts and parking facilities on the edge. In the town centre there will be a well-maintained church,. and towns usually have a pedestrian shopping area, a market square (with markets on Wednesdays and Saturdays), perhaps a cluster of half-timbered houses in an area of old cobbled streets, and a local museum (often free entry).

This apparent urban uniformity makes it easy for visitors to find their way round towns. Driving around the country, visitors will be surprised at how well hidden the industry is, giving an abiding impression that Denmark is still primarily an agricultural country.

What to See

The Essential rating system:

| ✓ | 'top ten' |

♦♦♦ do not miss
♦♦ see if you can
♦ worth seeing if
you have time

COPENHAGEN (KØBENHAVN)

Colourful and clean, friendly and fashionable, Copenhagen is a lively and compact city which is easy to explore. If you are used to walking about five miles (8km) a day it is best covered on foot – otherwise, you will need to take buses. For example, it is nearly two miles (3km) from the station to Rosenborg Palace and half a mile (1km) from the main hotel area to the Town Hall.
Copenhagen was the first city in Europe to ban cars and one of several pedestrianised areas is the mile-long (1.8km) **Strøget** (pronounced Stroit), which is the longest car-free street in Europe.
Copenhagen's architecture ranges from medieval brick buildings along winding streets to modern glass blocks beside six-lane highways. The inner city is clearly defined, and is divided by Strøget, running from **Rådhuspladsen** (Town Hall Square) in the west to **Kongens Nytorv** (the King's New Square) in the east. The oldest area is around Strøget

and includes the shady, cobbled square of Gråbrødretorv.
If it's hot you can stroll through one of the numerous parks or relax in an outdoor café and be entertained by youthful buskers, or you could take a waterside walk, perhaps to the famous, rather wistful statue of **den lille Havfrue** (the Little Mermaid). Copenhagen has a small canal network and a large harbour, but it's easy to forget that the city is by the sea until you suddenly come upon a forest of masts on **Nyhavn** canal. This was dug 300 years ago to encourage boats to sail nearer the city centre.
Apart from the parks, there are some lovely gardens – the large and tree-filled **Botanisk Have** (Botanical Gardens), and the delightful walled garden of the **Royal Library**. Some of Copenhagen's attractive monuments include the seated figure of **Hans Christian Andersen**, a fishwife by the former fishmarket, and the **Lurblowers** outside the Palace Hotel. There are many other figures, including the huge Gefion fountain.

Finding your Way

To get your bearings, tour the city by bus (HT Sightseeing lets you get on and off at nine stops), or better still, take a canal boat, starting from Gammel Strand or Holmens Kanal. But for a bird's-eye view there are several choices:

- the dome of Marmorkirken (Marble Church)
- the outside staircase of Vor Frelsers Kirke (closed in 1993)
- the viewing platform of Rundetårn (Round Tower)
- the Rådhus (Town Hall)
- the roof terrace of Illum department store.

History

Copenhagen began as a small fishing village (Havn) where the herring industry provided the main source of income. In the 12th century King Valdemar the Great handed Havn to Bishop Absalon of Roskilde, then the main city in Denmark, who built a fortress on Slotsholmen island to keep away marauding raiders. (Today the remains can be seen under Christiansborg Palace.) Over the next 200 years the town grew and became an important commercial centre, known as Købmands Havn (Merchants' Harbour), owned alternately by the king and the bishops. Erik of Pomerania imposed a toll on ships passing through the Øresund to increase the city's prosperity. Copenhagen became the capital city in 1443. Between 1600 and 1650, the city almost doubled in size when Christian 1V, the 'Builder King', created the canal area of Christianshavn and also bought land to the northeast to build his castles. His green-spired buildings remain an attractive legacy, but his extravagance impoverished the city.

Gefion and her transformed sons

The 18th century was disastrous for Copenhagen: it was badly damaged by two large fires and many people died in a plague. In the 1750s King Frederik V attempted to expand the city and designed some fine houses around Amalienborg. At the end of the century Copenhagen became embroiled in the Napoleonic Wars and the Battle of Copenhagen was fought against the English in 1801. Six years later the English came back, demanding the surrender of the Danish fleet, and bombarded the city.

The industrial revolution of the 19th century brought a sudden boost to the economy as factories and workers' houses were built. The city's ramparts came down in 1867 and were replaced by a string of parks.

ØSTERSØEN

Rønne
Bornholm

Country Distinguishing Signs

On the map above, international signs have been used to indicate the location of the countries which surround Denmark.

Thus:

D is Germany

S is Sweden

WHAT TO SEE

Castles

◆◆
AMALIENBORG PALACE
Amalienborg Slotsplads

This the residence of the Danish Royal family and is not open to the public. It was built around 1750 as part of Frederik V's grandiose scheme to expand Copenhagen. An equestrian statue of him stands in the centre of an octagonal courtyard, surrounded by four rococo palaces.

The best time to be there is noon, when, with complicated manoeuvres, the blue-uniformed (red on special occasions) guards change, having marched along the streets from Rosenborg Slot, accompanied by a band.

◆◆
CHRISTIANSBORG SLOT (PALACE)
Christiansborg Slotsplads

This complex of green-roofed buildings was constructed over Bishop Absalon's original 12th-century castle in the 1920s. To visit the Royal Reception Rooms you must take a conducted tour through opulent, empty rooms used only for state occasions, which are decorated with Italian chandeliers, silk wall coverings and ornamental plasterwork ceilings. In the same complex are the **Folketing** (Parliament – conducted tours only), the **Royal Stables** (in a surviving wing of an 18th-century palace) and the **Theatre Museum** with old costumes, dressing rooms and models of stage sets.

COPENHAGEN

◆◆◆
ROSENBORG SLOT ✓
(ROSENBORG CASTLE)

Østervoldgade 4A

Christian IV created Kongens Have (the King's Garden) in 1606 and within it built Rosenborg. This green-roofed extravaganza of spires and towers, surrounded by a moat and extensive park, was the home of the Danish royal family for nearly a century after its completion in 1633. The brick building, in Dutch Renaissance style, survived bombardments and fires and the exterior is unchanged.

Though exquisitely furnished, it is surprisingly informal, and shows the changing whims and fancies of the Danish monarchy. The rooms are arranged in chronological order: those from the time of Christian IV to Frederik IV have been faithfully preserved, while rooms from later periods have been accurately recreated.

The small rooms are packed with royal treasures – paintings, porcelain, Venetian glass, silver and ivory figures. The decorations include painted ceilings, Flemish tapestries, and an amber chandelier.

The most memorable rooms include the Winter Room with its Antwerp paintings, Frederik III's Marble Room, and Frederik IV's Mirror Cabinet, where the walls, ceiling and the centre of the floor are made of mirror glass. There is even a tiled bathroom, with running water, installed by Christian IV in 1616. The most magnificent room is the Long Hall, with stucco reliefs on the ceiling depicting political events of the time, two thrones guarded by silver lions, tapestries, Dutch fireplaces and silver mirrors. Finally, the tour descends to the basement where the crown jewels are kept – priceless pearls and diamonds, set in crowns, swords and mirrors, as well as an orb and sceptre.

Waterfront of the Nyhavn canal

Churches

HOLMENS KIRKE
Holmens Kanal
With its green copper tower and Dutch gable ends, this attractive old church was transformed from a forge by Christian IV. It was intended for the use of sailors – two model ships hang from the ceiling – a common feature of Danish churches. It has a Baroque oak reredos and a carved pulpit.

MARMORKIRKEN (MARBLE CHURCH)
Frederiksgade 4
This church was to be the centre of the new area around Amalienborg, planned during the reign of Frederik V, who laid the foundation stone in 1749. In 1770 the money ran out (the Norwegian marble was expensive) and the church was not completed until 1894. Statues of famous Danes stand inside and out.
The dome, one of the biggest in Europe – 90 feet (33m) in diameter – is supported on columns and decorated with coloured frescoes. You can go up to the gallery and out to the edge of the dome for far-reaching views.

VOR FRELSERS KIRKE (OUR SAVIOUR'S CHURCH)
Skt Annæ Gade
Completed in 1696, the interior of this church, with its gold starred vaulted ceiling, contains several angelic groups and the carved wooden organ case rests on two elephants.

The unusual exterior has a pale turquoise spire, around which curves an outside staircase guarded by railings (closed for repair in 1993). At the top stands the figure of Christ on a globe.

Museums

ARBEJDERMUSEET (WORKERS' MUSEUM)
Rømersgade 22
This educative and interesting Museum shows Copenhagen's social changes over the last century through reconstructions of three typical workers' homes and workplaces from the 1870s, 1930s and 1950s.
Old-style streets, backyards and workshops lead into a cramped home of the 1870s; the second flat is still very overcrowded, and the larger is a flat from the1950s.
For refreshment, visit the simple basement Cafe & Øl-Halle 1892 which serves food and beer from that era, or the 1930s Civic Restaurant. Both charge modern prices.

FRIHEDSMUSEET (RESISTANCE MUSEUM)
Churchillparken
Outside the museum stands the German armoured car in which the Danes brought news of the Nazi surrender. Inside, the museum graphically relates how initial civil resistance to the German occupation eventually turned to active sabotage. Tribute is paid to the British Royal Air Force who supplied radio transmitters and to those who smuggled out the Jews.

18

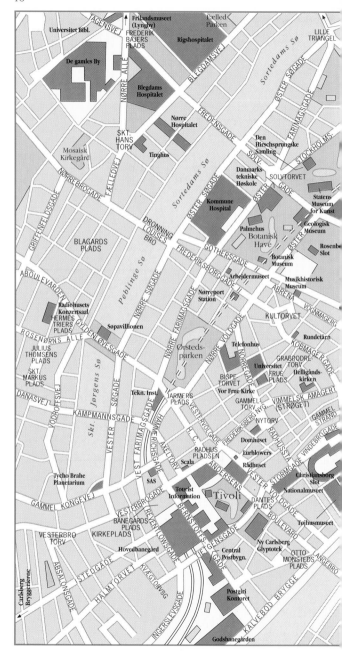

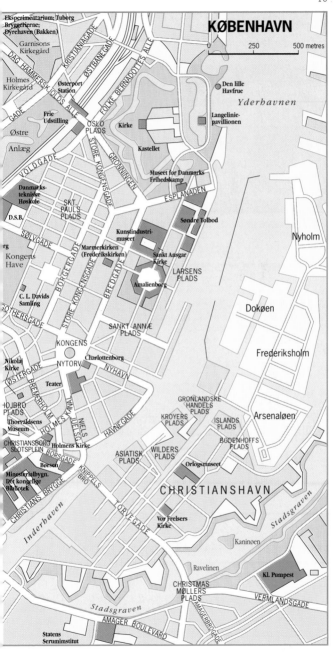

COPENHAGEN

Every little girl's dream

◆
HANS CHRISTIAN ANDERSEN
Nyhavn
Recently opened, and dedicated to Denmark's most famous writer, this is more of an activity centre than a museum, with musical entertainment, readings of his stories (in English) and displays of works of art connected with his life.

◆◆
DEN HIRSCHSPRUNGSKE SAMLING
(THE HIRSCHSPRUNG COLLECTION)
Stockholmsgade 20
Patron of the arts Heinrich Hirschsprung (1836–1908), a tobacco manufacturer, gave the nation his private collection of paintings, sculptures, drawings and water colours. The museum is housed in a charming building in a park. The works are by 19th- and 20th-century Danish artists; many designed the furniture. Paintings by Eckersberg, Købke and Lundbye represent the Golden Age; the Skagen and Funen painters are also there.

◆◆◆
NATIONALMUSEET
(THE NATIONAL MUSEUM)
Ny Vestergade 10
This vast museum is divided into five sections from the prehistoric to the present day and is particularly strong on the Bronze Age and the Vikings. However, it is currently being rebuilt and expanded and some sections (the Danish Folk Museum and the Collection of Near Eastern and Classical Antiquities) will not be rehoused until after 1994. Highlights include a tiny Bronze Age chariot (1400BC) pulling a golden disc representing the sun, and Danish domestic interiors which show how different strata of society lived from the 17th century. The Victorian Home (Klunkehjem), occupied by one family for 50 years from 1892, is fun to visit. A fascinating section on the Middle Ages includes displays of handicrafts, trades (old shoes and gold rings) and church interiors, as well as the Norsemen in Greenland. There is also a fine coin and medal collection from Greek times.

◆◆◆
NY CARLSBERG GLYPTOTEK
Dantes Plads 7
This museum houses the private classical collection of Carl Jacobsen from the Carlsberg brewery family, donated to the public in 1888. One of the most arresting features on the ground floor is a conservatory, with the *Water Mother* by the Danish sculptor, Kai Nielsen, set in a pond and framed by palms and lush

Deep green tranquillity at Ny Carlsberg Glyptotek

greenery. The largest room is the columned Banqueting Hall, in the style of a Greek temple, now used for concerts. It is ringed by sculpture galleries – mainly torsos and marble busts from Greece, Rome and the Near East. The Roman portraits are among the best in the world.

The Egyptian section has painted coffins and delightful bronze animals found in tombs. Work by 19th- and 20th-century Danish sculptors is on show, as well as works by Rodin, and there is a lively display of Etruscan art.

Two upper floors contain a valuable collection of later works – including bronze statuettes by Degas, and paintings from the Danish Golden Age and by French Impressionists, such as Monet, Pissarro and Cézanne.

◆◆◆
ORLOGSMUSEET (ROYAL DANISH NAVAL MUSEUM)
Overgaden oven Vandet 58A
Situated on the picturesque Christianshavn canal in a former naval hospital, the museum tells the story of the Danish Navy. The beautifully arranged exhibits show not only model and lifesize ships (including a 12-oar boat and the Royal Barge), but also portraits, weapons, naval artillery and many objects from shipwrecks.

◆◆◆
STATENS MUSEUM FOR KUNST (ROYAL MUSEUM OF FINE ARTS)
Sølvgade 48–50
This is Denmark's national gallery, housed in a large and stately building, and was founded in 1824 from works of art amassed by Danish kings. It holds a rich store of European masters, and the national collections of Danish art.

COPENHAGEN

◆◆
THORVALDSENS MUSEUM
Porthusgade 2
A distinctive polychrome
building which opened in 1848
to house the works of Bertel
Thorvaldsen (1770–1844), a
prolific sculptor whose fine
statues are found in many
European cities. He lived in
Rome for 40 years, and the
frieze on the building's exterior
depicts his return home and the
transport of his sculptures to the
museum.
Inside, the walls and ceilings
are in bold colours to show off
the statuary of larger-than-life
classical and biblical figures to
their best advantage. He
originally modelled in clay
which cracks when it dries, so
while it was still damp he
transformed his figures into
more stable plaster. Over many
years however, pollution has
discoloured many plaster
works and cleaning would
probably damage the surface.
Thovaldsen donated not only
the figures, drawings and
sketches to Copenhagen, but
also his library and collection of
paintings, coins, Roman and
Greek gems, bronzes and
vases.

◆◆
TØJHUSMUSEET
(THE ROYAL DANISH
ARSENAL MUSEUM)
Tøjhusgade 3
Officials in red jackets, black
tricorn hats and white gloves (a
modified version of late 16th-
century artillery uniform) greet
visitors to this museum which
shows the rise and fall of
Denmark's military power.
It is housed in Europe's longest
vaulted Renaissance hall, the
Cannon Hall, built around 1600,
and includes a fine collection of
muskets, gun carriages, cannon
balls and model sailing ships.
From 1648 the Museum stored
war trophies, and 200 years
later it became the repository of
the royal arms collection.

◆
TYCHO BRAHE
PLANETARIUM
Gammel Kongevej 10
The Planetarium, the largest in
Europe, is one of the city's
newest attractions. There are
'hands-on' models to help
visitors answer astronomical
questions, as well as films, and
laser displays are also given.

The beautiful Tivoli Gardens

Other Sights

◆◆
RUNDETÅRN (ROUND TOWER)
Købmagergade 52

On the initiative of King Christian IV this tower was built as an observatory in 1642, to be part of the new university complex. The King himself wrote the words on the gilded inscription, in rebus form. Around the edge of the viewing platform, nearly 96 feet (35m) above street level, runs a lovely wrought iron lattice.

Its unique feature is the ascent, a spiral ramp of 685 feet (209m) to enable the observatory equipment to be carried up. It is the oldest functioning observatory in Europe and is open to the public in winter. The original church and library were burnt down in 1728 (later rebuilt – the present church is a rococo delight), but the solid tower survived and the climb to the top is worth the effort.

◆◆◆
TIVOLI GARDENS

Centrally situated opposite the railway station, this amusement park-cum-pleasure gardens which was opened in 1843 is still immensely popular. From opening time (10.00hrs, end of April to mid-September only) when families and local pensioners arrive, until early evening when city workers drop by for a waffle, a sausage, or a glass of beer, the gardens continually buzz with activity and shrieks from the thrill rides. At dusk, thousands of coloured lamps lure in tourists for a meal or entertainment.

The successful ingredients are a pleasant setting – trees, lakes and a profusion of flowers – on which has been superimposed a large and irresistible funfair. There are nearly 30 restaurants, many exotically designed, a concert hall and theatres.

The Tivoli Guards, musically gifted boys aged 9 to 16, wearing bearskins, red jackets and white trousers (the uniform of the Queen's Life Guards), march through the Gardens at weekends and give free weekly concerts. Other free entertainment includes afternoon concerts, events on the open-air stage, evening ballet and mime at the Pantomime Theatre, and afternoon performances at the Children's Theatre. Stars of international repute play at the Concert Hall and Cabaret Theatre. Firework displays round off the evening three nights a week. In 1993, Tivoli celebrates its 150th birthday and a museum is opening to mark the occasion.

Tourist Information Office
The former office of the Copenhagen Tourist Information Office at the Tivoli entrance, is being taken over by the new Tivoli Museum. The new Information Office is at the corner of Bernstorffsgade 1 and Vesterbrogade, in the corner of Tivoli. The tourist office also incorporates the accommodation service.

COPENHAGEN

Entertainment

Copenhagen is the liveliest city in Scandinavia, not just Denmark, offering a wide choice of evening entertainment. All events are listed in the free monthly English publication *Copenhagen This Week*, available from the Tourist Office, hotels and the airport. Plays (sometimes in English) and ballet are performed at several theatres, and outside during the summer, in museum courtyards (at the **Kunstindustrimuseet**, for example). Concerts are staged at the **Radio House Concert Hall**, the **Royal Danish Academy of Music** and **Tivoli**. The opera and ballet seasons run from September to June on two stages of the **Royal Theatre**. A puppet theatre gives open-air shows in **Kongens Have**. There are many cinemas, and films are shown in the original language with Danish subtitles.

Live Music and Dancing

Copenhagen provides free music on summer weekends in **Amager Strandpark** (Saturday afternoons, rock) and in **Fælledparken** (Sundays). In the evenings, city bars, cafés and clubs, especially around **Vestergade**, throb with all kinds of music. Copenhagen is renowned for its jazz, and live bands perform in many places, including jazz restaurants. **Copenhagen Jazz House**, at Niels Hemmingsengade, has jazz nightly; **Cafeen Funke**, Skt Hans Torv (jazz, rock and blues) operates three nights a week. At **Hånd i Hanke**, Griffenfeldtsgade 20, bands play folk, blues and rock. **Montmartre**, Nørregade 41 is the largest venue with well-known local and international performers (there's a disco when the jazz stops) and **De Tre Musketerer**, Nikolaj Plads 25 offers traditional jazz most nights.

If you're lured into a nightclub by a pretty young girl, watch the prices. Unsuspecting tourists have been known to pay hundreds of kroner for a bottle of bubbly and the promise of a striptease.

Discos

Most start around midnight and carry on until the small hours. The atmosphere is casual and drink prices are reasonable. **Woodstock** at Vestergade 12 plays soul, rock and 60s music, and **U-Matic**, next door, is interesting. You're expected to be smartly dressed at **Daddy's**, Axeltorv 5, a large disco with a lightshow. **Sam's Bar**, Hovedvagtsgade 8 (and two places on Strøget, Østergade and Frederiksberggade) offers video karioke.

> ### Clubs
> As transient as popular taste, new clubs pop up, old ones disappear. For up-to-date information, ask at the tourist office or your hotel. The booklet *Wonderful Copenhagen by Night*, in Danish, German and English, suggests more places. Free disco tickets are often handed out in the streets.

Accommodation

Most visitors to Copenhagen come on a package tour, being allocated, or selecting from, a handful of hotels chosen by the tour operator. There is often a considerable price difference between rooms with and without private bathrooms. Independent travellers who don't want to spend too much could consider one of the following hotels which are all quite central; most only serve breakfast. The **Absalon** (tel: 31 24 22 11) in Helgolandsgade, behind the station, has nearly 500 beds and has recently been refurbished; it offers baby-sitting services. Two hotels very close to Rådhuspladsen, each with just over 100 beds, are **Hotel Alexandra** (tel: 33 14 22 00) with its own restaurant, and **Ascot Hotel** (tel: 33 12 60 00) with its own garage. A fairly new hotel is **Cab Inn** (tel: 31 21 04 00), in Danasvej (about five minutes by bus from Vesterport Station or by rail from Central Station). Bedrooms resemble a ship's cabin and are somewhat cramped, but they are clean

The Bazarbygningen

and cheap. A cafeteria service provides breakfast. For a family atmosphere, you could try **Ibsens Hotel** (tel: 33 13 19 13), run by three ladies, in the Frederiksborg district (northwest) of Copenhagen, about 10 minutes' bus ride from the centre; it has a garage. The accommodation service at the tourist office can (for a fee, currently DKr 13) arrange hotel, or (less expensive) private accommodation. However, in peak season it is advisable to book in advance, either direct with the hotel, or: Hotelbooking København, Bernstorffsgade 1, DK-1577 Copenhagen V.

Restaurants

With over 2,000 eating places in Copenhagen, visitors are spoilt for choice. By law, restaurants must display their prices, and there are no extras such as service charge. The city's restaurants – gourmet restaurants to bistros – are listed in *Copenhagen This Week*.

COPENHAGEN

The Lurblowers statue

Transport

Copenhagen runs an integrated bus and train system (*S-train*). The city is divided into zones, and a basic ticket (to be shown when changing bus or train within the hour) entitles you to one hour's travel on buses and S-trains. You pay extra for travel in more than two zones. If you are planning to make several journeys, it is cheaper to buy a two-, three-, five- or all-zones pass, each with ten strips valid for between one and two hours of travel; these must be stamped at the start of each journey at automatic machines just inside the bus or on the station platforms. Tickets can be used by several persons in the same party, if stamped accordingly.

For lunch, try a *smørrebrød*. **Ida Davidsen** (St Kongensgade 70) and **Kanal Cafeen** (Frederiksholms Kanal 18) specialise in them. Cellar restaurants such as **Lille Lækkerbisken** (34 Gammel Strand) and **Café Charlottenborg** (Nyhavn 2) provide a good lunch and a pleasant ambiance. A substantial two-course meal (*dagens ret*) can be bought in department stores such as **Illum**. For dinner, two good quality, but expensive fish restaurants are **Krogs Fiskerestaurant** (38 Gammel Strand) and **Den Gyldne Fortun** (Ved Stranden 18). Don't ignore the main railway station with its bars and restaurants, including the **Bistro** and **Grillen,** which specialise in Swedish salmon and roast beef. Slightly cheaper are **Sporvejen** (Gråbrødretorv 17) and **Galathea Kroen** (Rådhusstræde 9).

Copenhagen Card

Purhase of this card, for one, two or three days, entitles you to free travel on buses and S-trains within Copenhagen, and also on mainline trains and long distance buses within the whole of North Zealand, which includes Roskilde and Køge. It also gives you free admission to many attractions and museums, including the Louisiana Museum, a free tour on a sightseeing bus and 25 or 50 per cent discount on crossings to Sweden. An information booket about the museums and how to get to them is also issued free.
If you plan to do a lot of rail travel outside Copenhagen, this card is excellent value.

EXCURSIONS FROM COPENHAGEN

Dyrehaven (Deer Park) is a large area of trees and open parkland on the coast six miles (10km) north of Copenhagen, where herds of deer roam – some 300 years ago the area was a royal hunting ground . In one corner is Dyrehavsbakken, an amusement park familiarly known as **Bakken**. Open from the end of March to the end of August, it is older than Tivoli (and free), with over 100 fairground attractions. International artists often perform, there is a resident clown and around 30 restaurants.

Two attractive beaches north of town are **Bellevue** and **Charlottenlund Fort**. South of the city is **Køge Bugt Strandpark**.

> **On Mondays . . .**
> Monday is not a good day for sightseeing, because only a handful of museums, several churches and gardens, the Tivoli Gardens and the Round Tower are open.

Copenhagen's bustling Town Hall Square

EXCURSIONS FROM COPENHAGEN

◆◆
BRYGGERIERNE (BREWERIES)
Hellerup

Denmark's two largest breweries, Carlsberg and Tuborg, are now part of one company and each runs very popular free guided tours round their plants, which end with free samples.

The processes are highly automated, from steeping barley to bottling the beer and visitors are taken from one part of the plant to another by bus. At Tuborg they are shown the 85-foot (26m) bottle built for an industrial exhibition in 1888 which holds the equivalent of 1.5 million ordinary bottles.

◆
EKSPERIMENTARIUM
Hellerup

This new science centre near the Tuborg Brewery is very popular with young Danes because it gives them the opportunity to experiment – test their blood pressure or sense of balance, for example, or link up with a weather computer. As the instructions are almost entirely in Danish, it is difficult for foreign visitors to participate!

◆◆
FRILANDSMUSEET
Lyngby

Frilandsmuseet is an open-air museum set in the wooded countryside at Lyngby, some eight miles (13km) north of Copenhagen.

Nearly 50 old Danish farms and cottages from the 17th to the 19th centuries have been dismantled, moved and reassembled here, complete with flocks of sheep and geese. All the buildings have been authentically furnished in different regional styles. Threshing and weaving demonstrations recreate old-style rural life.

Watch Out for Cyclists
When stepping off a bus in any Danish city, look carefully to the right first, as there is a cycle track between the road and the pavement along which they soundlessly pedal.

A tall ship on Copenhagen's Nyhavn canal is a reminder of the graceful days of sail

FUNEN (FYN)

The smallest of Denmark's
three large islands, Funen is the
prettiest, particularly in the
south, where the flatness gives
way to rolling hills and an
attractive archipelago. Apart
from an industrial area north of
Odense, the island's main town,
Funen, is agricultural,
producing most of Denmark's
fruit and vegetables. The
countryside is dotted with
grand manor houses, thatched
cottages and country towns.
The sea is calm and shallow, so
safe for children, and many
beaches have the EC Blue Flag
award. The best are west of
Bogense and along the northeast coast as far as Nyborg.
The eastern side of the northern
tip of Hindsholm is also
attractive.

Getting There

Funen is acccessible by road
(E20) across the bridge from
Jutland to Middelfart, and from
the island of Langeland.
There are also ferries to
Zealand, to other offshore
islands and to Germany
(Fåborg to Gelting and
Langeland to Kiel).
In the mid-1990s the Storebælt
(Great Belt) Bridge, one of the
world's largest construction
projects, together with a tunnel,
will link Knudshoved to
Halsskov, on Zealand.
Exhibition centres at either end
of the construction site have
models, videos and drawings
illustrating how the work is
progressing – the Knudshoved
Exhibition is rumoured to be
the better one.

WHAT TO SEE

◆◆◆
EGESKOV ✓

The eccentric Egeskov Castle

This private home is a romantic,
turretted castle, which claims to
be the best-kept Renaissance
island castle in Europe. Its most
attractive moated setting is
matched by its beautiful
interior, perhaps somewhat
contrived as the rooms have
been specially arranged to fit a
theme or period, rather than
being left as they were.
The castle, finished in 1554, was
built on a foundation of oak
piles driven in to the lake –
Egeskov means oak forest –
and apparently a whole forest
was used. The thick walls hide
secret staircases, a well and
chimneys. Jagstuen (the
Hunting Room) and Jagtgangen
(the Hunting Corridor) may not
appeal to animal lovers – they
are full of trophies, including a
lion, a cheetah and elephant
tusks, killed by a former owner,
Count Gregers Ahlefeldt–
Laurvig–Bille. The huge,
beamed Riddersalen (Knights'
Hall) is empty except for its

large paintings, but is often used for concerts.

The castle contains much fine furniture and art, and many tiled ovens. The roof was recently repaired, and in the roofspace is a display of the plans and photos; you get a great view of the grounds, too. Highlights here are displays of fuchsias, the fountains and a bamboo maze. **Veteranmuseum** is an impressive collection of old cars and aircraft, and in a large barn is **Hestevogns og Landbrugsmuseum** (Horse and Carriage and Agricultural Museum) with old farm machinery and implements. Egeskov is at Kværndrup, about 15.5 miles (25km south-east of Odense.

Fåborg's carillon plays hymns daily

◆◆◆
FÅBORG

The centre of this little town is delightful, like a living museum, with photo-opportunities galore amongst its cobbled streets lined with picturesque buildings. Situated on the south-west coast of Funen, the town belonged, at various times, to both Denmark and Schleswig: in the 18th century it owned one of the largest fleets in Denmark and was an important trading town. Today, boats ply to Gelting (Germany) and to nearby Danish islands (Ærø, Lyø and Avernakø).

Sightseeing

Den Gamle Gård (The Old Merchant's House) was built in 1725, and once belonged to Mr Voigt, whose daughter was an early love of Hans Andersen. Now it recreates life around 1800 in a series of rooms, from the kitchen, with its boxbed for the maid and hatch for the brooding goose, to the grander master's bedroom. Other rooms display glass, china, textiles and local gravestones.

Fåborg Museum of Funen Painting exhibits pictures, predominantly local landscapes by the famous Funen painters, including Peter Hansen, Johannes Larsen and Fritz Syberg during the years 1880–1920. There are also portraits, still life and seascapes as well as powerful paintings by Kristian Zahrtmann, who strongly influenced the Funen group. They selected and sold their paintings to wine-factory owner Mads Rasmussen, who helped establish this museum.

Klokketårnet (the clock tower) is Fåborg's landmark, and has Funen's largest carillon. Its church is long since gone but two others remain: **Horne Kirke**, a 12th-century round church with a crucifix from the Middle Ages and a font made by Thorvaldsen, and **Helligåndskirken** (Church of the Holy Ghost), originally built as part of a monastery – King Christian's Bible lies on the altar.

Excursions from Fåborg

Outside Fåborg are two mills: one at **Grubbe**, to the west, restored and operating, the other northeast at **Kaleko**, very much older and furnished to show a miller's lifestyle.

Accommodation

In town, **Hotel Strandgade** (tel: 62 61 20 12) offers comfortable accommodation while the half-timbered **Youth Hostel** at Grønnegade 71–2 is one of the most popular in Denmark (tel: 62 61 12 03).

The modern **Hotel Faaborg Fjord** (tel: 62 61 10 10) is just over a mile (2km) southeast of the town by the harbour. It stands in its own grounds and is elegantly furnished.

Two places near Fåborg are full of character. **Steensgård Herregårdspension** (tel: 62 61 94 90) at Millinge, northwest of Fåborg, is a grand moated manor house set in a park. In contrast, **Faldsled Kro**, in the pretty village of Faldsled, is a group of thatched buildings by the sea, with an attractive garden (tel: 62 68 11 11). Both hotels serve excellent meals.

Restaurants

The atmospheric **Mouritz** is on Østergade, the main street, is open daily for long hours, while **Ved Brønden**, in the square, specialises in fish dishes. **Tre Kroner**, near the harbour (Strandgade 1) has been in business for nearly 200 years.

NYBORG

Nyborg is an old harbour town on the east of Funen, on the historic trading route between Jutland and Zealand – a role which will continue when the new Storebælt (Great Belt) Bridge linking Funen to Zealand is completed; there is an exhibition centre at the construction site. In medieval times, it was the capital of Denmark, and it has succeeded in preserving some of its past in spite of damage inflicted during the wars against Sweden and by occupying Spanish troops in the Napoleonic Wars. More recently, several rather intrusive modern buildings have been constructed amongst the old houses and cobbled streets.

Sightseeing

The oldest surviving building is **Nyborg Slot** (the Castle), founded in 1170 as part of a chain of coastal forts to fend off Denmark's enemies. In the Middle Ages, Danish kings lived and held court here. The castle is partly surrounded by water, and in the restored wing (Knudstårn) there are fortress remains and a weapon collection. **Landporten** (the Town Gate) dates from 1660 is the oldest in Denmark and forms part of the original ramparts.

Another fine old medieval building is **Mads Lerches Gård**, now the Nyborg Regional Museum. In the two-storey, half-timbered house, the rooms have been laid out so as to show the lifestyle of a rich merchant.

Vor Frue Kirke (Church of our Lady) was founded in 1388.

Close by is **Korsbrødregården**, once part of a monastery, whose Gothic arched cellar is now a shop.

Accommodation and Restaurants

Hesselhuset (tel: 65 31 24 48) is a restaurant with good views across the Great Belt, and **Hotel Nyborg Strand** (tel: 65 31 31 31) is a large hotel in its own grounds.

◆◆◆
ODENSE ✓

Funen's main town and Denmark's third largest, Odense is famous as the birthplace of the writer of fairytales, Hans Christian Andersen. It derives its name from the Norse god, Odin. In the Middle Ages the town attracted pilgrims to Skt Albani Kirke (St Alban's Church) where King Knud (Canute) was murdered and later canonised. Odense has always been an important trading town, and when a canal was dug to Kerteminde, the town's commercial future was assured. Today, the city is sliced in two by the main road (01), and is dominated by the huge skyscraper block of Sparekassen Bikuben Fyn. Exploring the town on foot, it becomes apparent that today's citizens are desperately trying to make amends for the destruction they and their forebears wrought, by carefully restoring the surviving old buildings and creating some superb museums.

The city is well endowed with parks, and there is a lovely riverside walk along the edge of Odense Å (River Odense).

Sightseeing

Brandts Klædefabrik, Brandts Passage 37–43, once a cloth mill and Odense's largest workplace, has been cleverly refurbished to become Denmark's first international art and cultural centre. In the four-storey building (no lift) are an art gallery (**Kunsthallen**),

cinemas, two museums, and live entertainment takes place in the courtyard (Amphitheater).

In **Danmarks Grafiske Museum** (Danish Museum of Printing) at Brandts is a range of old machines showing the development of the printing industry over the last 300 years. Every morning retired workers demonstrate their skills in lithography, bookbinding and other processes. The Pressemuseum catalogues the history of the Danish press from 1666. As well as a rotary printing press, the museum has yellowed copies of regional newsapers, many showing evidence of the censors. A typical editor's office around 1900, with old-style phone and typewriter, can be compared with a modern one with a desk-top computer and an overflowing ashtray.

The second museum at Brandts, **Museet for Fotokunst** (Museum of Photographic Art), has a permanent photo collection and various temporary exhibitions.

Carl Nielsen Museet is appropriately situated adjoining the Odense Concert Hall, Claus Bergs Gade II, and traces the life (1865–1931) of this composer of operas, symphonies and popular songs, born near Odense. He married the gifted sculptress Anne Marie, whose work is also displayed.

As well as mementoes of their European travels, programmes and scores of Nielsen's works, his medals, and reports of his almost state funeral, are recreations of their cluttered rooms – her studio, his music room – all viewed to the accompaniment of the composer's music. Headphones are available and there is a video show.

Fyns Kustmuseum (Funen Art Museum), Jernbanegade 13, in a classical building erected less than a century ago, contains pictures by Danish artists from Jens Juel to Asger Jorn, including the Funen painters, active at the turn of the century. A section displays sculpture and Constructivist art.

Both the museums devoted to Hans Christian Andersen may come as a disappointment, particularly to children. **Hans Christian Andersens Barndomshjem** (Childhood Home), Munkemøllestræde 3–5, is a small, unfurnished two-roomed cottage now dwarfed by modern buildings, where the writer lived from 1807 to 1819.

Instead of items asssociated with Andersen's childhood, it contains early photos and plans of the house and the surrounding area, one letter written by him and a wood engraving.

The much larger museum, **Hans Christian Andersens Hus**, Hans Jensens Stræde 37–45 is in a heavily restored area of cobbled streets and pretty cottages. Andersen was born here in 1805, and the cottage has been extended to accommodate the books and other materials pertaining to his life.

The exhibition demands a lot of reading – of his poems, travel notes and early manuscripts.

Illustrations of his tales are displayed, as are some of his paper cut-outs.

A reconstruction of his room shows old furniture, pictures and personal possessions – hatbox, suitcase and boots. In a circular memorial hall the walls are decorated with scenes from his life, and in the library are volumes of his works in many languages.

A slide show, with commentary, narrates his life story and headphones enable visitors to listen to some of his well-known tales.

Jernbanemuseet (Railway Museum) adjoining Odense station is a popular attraction, with its luxurious royal carriages and a turn-of-the-century station. The museum, extended and modernised in 1988, illustrates the history of the Danish railway from 1847, with actual trains and locomotives, and a big model railway track.

Møntergården, Overgade 48–50, is a delightful museum of cultural and urban history set in a collection of 16th- and 17th-century buildings.

As well as recreating medieval Odense through finds and photographs from excavations, the museum presents older reconstructed buildings, including St Alban's wooden church, and a Dominican abbey with realistic tableaux of monks at work. The coin and medal collection is said to be the finest in the country.

There is a new toy exhibition, a display of women's clothing, and a number of embroidered samplers.

Skt Knuds Domkirke (St Canute's Cathedral), Flakhaven, is a lofty Gothic edifice dating from about 1300. The finely carved gold and black altarpiece, by the 16th-century Lübeck craftsman Claus Berg, together with the stained glass window, adds colour to the white interior. In the crypt are the remains of King Canute, killed in St Albans Church; the contents of a second coffin are disputed – either Canute's brother Benedict or St Alban himself, brought back to Denmark by Canute. Hans Christian Anderson was confirmed here.

Skt Hans Kirke, Nørregade, was started a bit later as an abbey church and is the only Danish church with an exterior pulpit. The interior is vaulted, has a carved pulpit and frescos.

Skt Knuds Domkirke

Accommodation

Odense's popularity on account of Hans Andersen, and as a conference centre, means that hotel standards are high, as are the prices. Two cheaper hotels are the centrally located **Ydes Domir** (tel: 66 12 11 31), an old building, recently extended, and the much smaller **Kahema** (tel: 66 12 28 21), with only 14 rooms and no showers en suite. Another option is to stay outside Odense. **Mørkenborg Kro og Motel**, founded in 1771, (tel: 64 83 10 51), is at Veflinge, 11 miles (18km) northwest of Odense, in lovely surroundings. **Bogense Hotel** (tel: 64 81 11 08) in Bogense, a coastal market town about 18.5 miles (30km) from Odense, is comfortable with good food.

Restaurants

Restaurants proliferate, not only along the streets, but also in museums, and in the shopping complex at Rosengårdcentret. One of the prettiest is **Under Lindetræt**, in a half-timbered house near Hans Andersen's Museum, which serves nouvelle cuisine (tel: 66 12 92 86).

Den Gamle Kro (Overgade 23) is also central, with a courtyard (tel: 66 12 14 33).

Restaurant Zander prides itself on its fresh food (evening meals only) in unpretentious surroundings (tel: 66 12 50 92).

Entertainment

There's a variety of nightlife in Odense – get the most up-to-date information from the tourist office.

Serious-minded visitors can hear the Odense Symphony Orchestra in the new **Concert Hall**. Odense has several theatres, the largest is the **Odense Theatre** (plays are performed in Danish only). Jazz lovers can enjoy the summer programme *Sommerjazz med Fyn og Klem* and for rock fans there are free outdoor concerts. Other vibrant light entertainment includes: jazz pubs, night clubs, bars and discos.

The **Atlantic Night Club** (Overgåde 45–7) has a disco. Upmarket jazz is played at the **Cotton Club**, Pantheonsgåde 5C. Odense's casino is at the **H C Andersen Hotel**.

Excursions from Odense

Boats cruise from Munke Mose Park along willow-tree lined banks to Fruens Bøge, from where you can walk to Funen Village (see below), or you can disembark earlier at Tivoli or the zoo.

Further afield, a 16th-century manor house and its more recent outbuildings, southeast of Odense, is now a cultural centre (**Kulturcenter Hollufgård**), standing in extensive woodlands and meadows. One of the most important buldings is **Fyns Oldtid-Hollufgård** (Funen Prehistory Museum) which displays local archaeological finds in an exciting way. On the first floor there is the storehouse, a vast collection of early finds from Funen – stones, buckles, spearheads and pots – available to all visitors, particularly local amateur archaeologists.

Outside, a prehistoric trail and landscape have been created, with thatched houses from Viking and Bronze Age times; examples from the Stone and Iron Ages are to follow soon. Sculptures are displayed in the park and there is a sculpture workshop. There are also two golf courses and nature trails.

Den Fynske Landsby (Funen Village) is an attractive open-air museum where about 25 thatched buildings from rural Funen (dating mostly from the 18th and 19th centuries) have been relocated to form a village, complete with homes, a school, a smithy and an almshouse, all furnished in period style. Old farming and cattle-raising methods are employed. In summer, potters and other craftspeople demonstrate their skills, and the

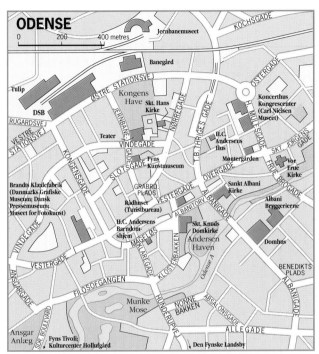

charming Hans Christian
Andersen play is performed by
children on the open-air stage
between mid-July and early
August.

Travel

Local buses are red; long-
distance ones are red or
yellow. Get on at the back,
alight at the front. Different
sorts of tickets are available.
If your journey entails two or
more buses, and will take less
than an hour, ask for an
omstigning (transfer ticket).
A two-day *eventyr pas*
(adventure pass) is worth
buying, and can be obtained
from tourist offices, museums

and hotels, from campsites and
the railway station – and gives
free entry to 13 museums
(including all those listed
above), the zoo, a guided tour
of the town hall, swimming
pools, and a free river trip. The
pass provides free travel on
red and yellow buses and on
some local trains.

◆◆
SVENDBORG

Superbly situated on the Sound
at the southeast corner of
Funen, Svendborg is the natural
gateway to the island of
Tåsinge and to the pretty South
Funen archipelago; it also
makes a good base from which

to explore inland Funen. Yachtsmen come here in large numbers every summer and Svendborg is the starting place for *Fyn rundt*, the annual wooden ships' race around the island.

Scenically, Svendborg is dominated by its busy harbour: Funen's agricultural products are exported from here and the shipyard is the biggest employer. One of the town's biggest factories produces cornflakes for Scandinavia.

Sightseeing

The winding streets go down quite steeply to the harbour, passing between many old half-timbered houses. The grandest is **Anne Hvide's Gård** which dates from about 1560, prominently standing near the main square. Now part of the **Svendborg og Omegns Museum** (Svendborg County Museum), the rooms are furnished in the styles of 1700 and 1800, with portraits and collections of clocks and stoves. Another part of the museum is housed in **Viebæltegård**, the town's former poorhouse, and includes craft workshops (coir mats are still made), local archaeological finds and an apartment from the 1950s.

The **Zoological Museum** shows the range of Danish animals since the Ice Age, as well as a more recent skeleton – that of a whale, beached locally.

Although Svendborg can trace its history back 700 years, and

Colourful barns relocated at Den Fynske Landsby open-air museum

still retains its mill pond, only one church preserves any ancient remains – **Skt Nikolai**, built of large, medieval bricks, with a 16th-century tower and a Skovgaard-painted altar. **Vor Frue Kirke** was orignally Romanesque, but was later rebuilt in Gothic style. It is the prettier and more homely of the two, with a Dutch carillon.

Accommodation

Christiansminde is a new holiday centre (self-catering as well as a hotel), near woods and beaches and ideal for families (tel: 62 21 90 00). **Hotel Ærø** (tel: 62 21 07 60) is a smaller hotel by the harbour. More costly but central is **Hotel Svendborg** (tel: 62 21 17 00)

Restaurants

All the hotels mentioned above have good restaurants, but you could also try **Restaurant Borgen** (tel: 62 21 30 40), a lovely building with sea views.

Entertainment

Several places have live music, including **Børsen Restaurant** once a week, and **Bodegåden**, in Brogade, at weekends. **Under Uret** is a popular pavement café/pub full of old clocks.

Excursions from Svendborg

The old ship *Helge*, built in 1924, sails via the island of Thurø to Valdemars Slot on Tåsinge, five times a day in summer – it takes about an hour. Other ferries go to the nearby tiny islands of Drejø, Skaro, and Hjortø, and to the larger island of Ærø (see **Funen's Islands**, overleaf).

FUNEN'S ISLANDS

The area around Svendborg is
a paradise for yachting
enthusiasts, and many of the
islands have well equipped
marinas.
Note that public transport is
limited.

WHAT TO SEE

DREJØ
The largest of the three, 1,018
acres (412 hectares), has few
trees after a fire 50 years ago,
which also destroyed some
timber-framed houses. But it
has a 16th-century church, a
grocer's shop, and a restaurant.

SKARØ
This is mainly a bird reserve,
with salt meadows and fields
which are triangular as a result
of the enclosure movement.
There is one village, and a grill-
bar but no restaurant.

HJORTØ
This is the smallest of the three,
also with wonderful birdlife.
Cars and motorbikes are not
allowed, and if you want to stay
the night you will need to bring
a tent.

LANGELAND
An elongated, mostly flat,
cultivated island, Langeland has
excellent child-friendly sandy
beaches, backed by grass-
covered dunes, particularly the
northern tip, the eastern coast
and at Ristinge in the southwest.
The island is popular with

holidaymakers and has two
holiday centres as well as
hotels, campsites and lots of
summerhouses. Many of the
private gardens are beautifully
maintained – a local tradition.
Evidence of early settlement is
seen in the many prehistoric
burial mounds.
Rudkøbing, the main town, was
700 years old in 1987 and its
timber-framed houses, 18th-
century buildings and winding
streets contribute to its charm.
The port is a hive of activity, but
while the new yachting marina
flourishes, the commercial
harbour declines. Fish is sold
on the quayside.
Langeland has good links to
other islands: ferries to Strynø
and Ærø (from Rudkøbing), to
Zealand (from Lohals), to
Lolland (from Spodsbjerg), and
to Kiel in Germany (from
Bagenkop) and a bridge to
Tåsinge.

Sightseeing
The collection in the **Langeland
Museum** includes numerous
prehistoric finds, from the Stone
Age onwards. A prized
possession is a 2,000-year-old
bronze receptacle, and there is
also Renaissance fishing
equipment and items belonging
to famous locals. In **det gamle
Apotek** (the old pharmacy) is a
rare collection of chemists'
equipment. Another part of the
museum (at Østergade 25)
concentrates on fishing and
sailing. The pretty red-brick
step-gabled 12th-century
church has gated pews with
painted biblical texts.
Sightseeing on the rest of the
island is limited to **Tranekær**,

where the **Slotsmølle** (Castle
Mill) still produces flour and has
an exhibition on mill history.
The moated red-coloured
castle, set on a mound, was
reconstructed in the last
century but is not open; the
surrounding park is. Tranekær
village, with its half-timbered
houses, is most attractive.

Accommodation and
Restaurants
Dageløkke Kro, about five
miles (8km) north of Tranekær
is a charming old inn (tel: 62 59
13 01). **Tranekær
Gæstgivergård** (tel: 62 59 12
04), near the castle is very
comfortable, and in Rudkøbing,
Hotel Rudkøbing Skudehavn
(tel: 62 51 46 00) is in a lovely
position by the harbour.

◆◆
THURØ
A pretty little rural island,
accessible from Svendborg by
a causeway. Apart from a
castle, there is little to do but
enjoy the countryside and the
beaches.
The only hotel is **Hotelpension
Røgeriet** (tel: 62 20 50 84), but
you can find bed and breakfast
places.

The windswept island of Langeland

◆◆◆
TÅSINGE
Connected by bridges to both
Funen and Langeland, it is easy
to drive over Tåsinge without
stopping – but that would be a
shame. It's a pretty island, hilly
in the north, quite flat in the
south, but intensely cultivated
and dotted with thatched
houses and clumps of trees.

Sightseeing
In the little coastal village of
Troense, with streets of half-
timbered houses, is an
outstanding castle and a
maritime museum.
The castle is **Valdemars Slot
Herregårdsmuseum** (locally
called the Funen Manor House
Museum), and was built in late
baroque style by Christian IV
for his son, Valdemar. In 1678
the estate was bought and
extended by Niels Juel, the
naval hero. The main building
overlooks a lake. The grand,
spacious rooms have gilded
plasterwork, and include a
banqueting hall, library and
chapel. Tapestries and a fine art
collection cover the walls, and
much of the beautiful furniture

is French. The **Maritime Collection**, a branch of the Svendborg Museum, is in the old village school. The exhibition explains the importance of the sailing ship era; there are also paintings, model ships, wooden figureheads and sailors' souvenirs.

Just south of Troense, the tower of Bregninge church provides a good view.

Accommodation and Restaurants

Hotel Troense (tel: 62 22 54 12) is in the village overlooking the sea; and Bregninge Kro (tel: 62 22 54 75), is a century-old inn. Both serve meals, as does Lodskroen Restaurant in Troense.

♦♦♦
ÆRØ ✓

The Danes call this island 'the green pearl' in the south Funen archipelago – the jewel in the crown might be more apt. Slightly larger than Tåsinge, but long and thin rather than circular, it presents an attractive hilly landscape dotted with farms, windmills and burial mounds. The west coast is straight, and steep in the south, while the east is indented with bays and coves. Best bathing beaches are Vester at Ærøskøbing, Jørbæk at Søby, and Risemark facing the Baltic. Several ferry services sail to Ærø's three harbours from other islands: to Marstal from Rudkøbing (on Langeland); to Ærøskøbing from Svendborg

Aerial view of Ærøskøbing

and to Søby from Fåborg (both on Funen); and to Søby from Mommark (on Als island) during the summer. The prettiest route is from Svendborg, and passes many small islands.

Sightseeing

Ærøskøbing is the wonder of Ærø. It is a perfectly preserved urban layout, its colour-washed timber-framed houses – some leaning dangerously – date from the 17th and 18th centuries. They cover an extensive area, and visitors strolling through the cobbled streets feel they have stepped back in time. Denmark's oldest post office, dating from 1749, still functions.

The few museums are small but give visitors a chance to enter these old, tiny-windowed buildings. **Ærø Museum**, in the former bailiff's house tells the history of the island from prehistoric times through locally found items. Displays include textiles, domestic articles, a maritime collection and the interior of the old apothecary. An unusual museum is the **Flaskeskibs-samlingen** (Bottle Ship Collection), also called 'Bottle Peter', where hundreds of old model ships in bottles are displayed together with newer ones made by the late owner, sea captain Peter Jacobsen. In the same building is Hans Billedhuggers Mindestuer (memorial rooms), with examples of his folk art and carvings.

Hammerichs Hus is an 18th-century merchant's house with locally made glass, furniture, tiles and china.

Attractive villages worth visiting on Ærø include **Ommel**, with a tiny harbour and thatched cottages, and **Store Rise**, the location of Ærø's oldest church founded in the 12th century, with a medieval monastery gate. **Bregninge** village in the northwest has a very long main street and a beautiful 13th-century church. Inside are frescos, and a triptych carved by Claus Berg.

On the coast, **Vodrup Klint** (cliffs), west of Tranderup, provides unusual scenery of large slopes; a footpath leads to the beach. **Marstal**, an old maritime town, is now the largest settlement on Ærø. The granite jetty dates from the last century, and wooden boats are still made in the shipyard. The town has a few cobbled streets but a large number of new houses impinges on the old. **Marstal Søfartsmuseum** (Maritime Museum) shows many models of ships, navigation equipment and sailors' souvenirs.

Accommodation

Two pleasant family hotels in the old part of Ærøskøbing, each with a garden, are **Hotel Ærøhus** (tel: 62 52 10 03) and **Det Lille Hotel** (tel: 62 52 23 00). **Bregninge Kro** is an old inn by Bregninge church (tel: 62 58 18 14).

Restaurants

The hotels listed above have good dining rooms. Another place to try is **Vindeballe Kro** (tel: 62 52 16 13), a charming old country inn.

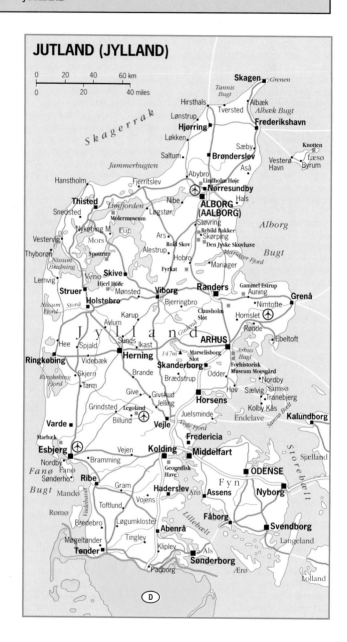

JUTLAND (JYLLAND)

0   20   40   60 km
0   20   40 miles

Skagerrak

Skagen — *Grenen*

Hirsthals
Tannis Bugt
Tversted
Albæk
Albæk Bugt
Frederikshavn

Lønstrup
Hjørring

Løkken

Saltum
Sæby
Brønderslev

Knotten
Vesterø Havn — *Læsø* Byrum

Jammerbugten

Abybro
Lindholm Høje
Nørresundby
Hals

Hanstholm
Fjerritslev
Nibe
ÅLBORG (AALBORG)
Aså

Thisted
Limfjorden
Løgstør
Støvring
Rebild Bakker
Skørping
Den Jyske Skovhave

Alborg

Sneδsted
Nykøbing M
Mølemuseum
Fur
Ars
Rold Skov
Alestrup

Bugt

Vestervig
Mors
Spøttrup
Hobro
Mariager Fjord

Thyborøn
Nissum Bredning
Skive
Hjerl Hede
Fyrkat
Mariager

Lemvig
Veno
Mønsted
Viborg
Randers
Gammel Estrup
Auning

Struer
Storà
Holstebro
Bjerringbro
Nimtofte
Grenå

Nissum Fjord
Karup
Clausholm Slot
Horristet

Avlum
Sunds
Ikast
Gudenà
Rønde
Ebeltoft

Hee
Spjald
ÅRHUS
Arhus Bugt

Ringkøbing
Videbæk
Herning
Skanderborg
Marselisborg Slot
Forhistorisk Museum Moesgård

Ringkøbing Fjord
Skjern
Brande
Odder
Nordby

Tarm
Brædstrup
Høv
Sælvig
Samsø
Tranebjerg

Give
Givskud
Jelling
Legoland
Horsens
Kolby Kås

Grindsted
Billund
Vejle
Juelsminde
Endelave
Kalundborg

Varde
Tefte Fjord

Marbæk
Esbjerg
Vejen
Kolding
Fredericia
Middelfart

Nordby
Bramming
Geografisk Have

Sjælland

Fanø Fanø
Sønderho
Ribe
Fyn
ODENSE

Bugt
Mandø
Gram
Haderslev
Arø Assens
Nyborg

Toftlund
Vojens

Romø
Vadehavet
Løgumkloster
Fåborg

Bredebro
Åbenrå
Lillebælt
Svendborg

Møgeltønder
Tingley
Kliplev
Als
Langeland

Tønder
Sønderborg

Padborg
Ærø
Lolland

Storebælt

(D)

A strategically placed stork's nest

JUTLAND (JYLLAND)

This aptly named peninsula is about 250 miles (400km) from north to south and includes almost every type of European terrain on a miniature scale. The south is marshy grazing land, and dotted with pretty towns whose history is closely linked to that of Schleswig–Holstein in Germany. Many market towns maintain their strong cattle-raising tradition and still hold cattle fairs and tilting tournaments.

Mid-Jutland's landscape includes lakes and moors inland, and on the coast, wide beaches of white sand and lagoons. Off the tapering northern tip of Denmark (the Skaw) is the unusual spectacle of two seas colliding. Here the wind has created sand dunes and beaches along the coast. In this ancient part of Europe, human influence on the landscape dates back to the Stone Age, and Viking graves, Bronze Age burial mounds and recreated homesteads may be seen. Three of Denmark's largest towns are on Jutland, but their total population is less than half a million people.

WHAT TO SEE

◆◆◆
BILLUND

Billund is a small village dominated by the airport, **Legoland** (see page 51), and now by **Museumscenter Billund**, opened in 1990 and within walking distance of the airport. The huge white building houses a trio of transport collections.

Danmarks Flyvemuseum (Aviation Museum) covers 80 years of aviation and includes Ellehammer's aeromachine (1906) and information on the development of aircraft engines, space research and meteorology.

Danmarks Bilmuseum (Car Museum) exhibits over 70 gleaming cars and a good collection of motor-cycles. Denmark's own car pioneer, Jørgen Skafte Rasmussen, who founded DKW, has a special stand. **Falck Museet**, named after its founder, shows past and present rescue equipment used by the fire and ambulance services. Frogmen and firemen give occasional demonstrations.

###
CLAUSHOLM

Clausholm Slot (Castle) is a five-winged baroque mansion built at the beginning of the 18th century for the then Lord Chancellor, Count Conrad Rewentlow. His daughter Anna Sophie eloped with Frederik IV and became Queen; after his death in 1730 she lived at Clausholm with her court. The richly furnished rooms have elaborate stucco ceilings and decorated panels. In the chapel, unchanged since the Queen's time, is Denmark's oldest organ. The extensive grounds include a number of fountains.

◆◆
EBELTOFT

The name means 'Apple Orchard' and apple trees still flourish in this charming seaside market town, one of the most attractive in Denmark. Long, cobbled streets parallel to the shore are lined with timber-framed houses, many over 200 years old. Several are now shops, and while the pottery, patchwork and picture shops fit easily into this rural setting, those selling videos, sports wear and milkshakes seem incongruous.

Sightseeing

Ebeltoft has a long history and claims its 16th-century town hall, now a one-room museum, is the smallest in the world. In summer two uniformed nightwatchmen, with spiked mace and lantern, sing old songs on the town hall steps.

The frescoed church dates from the 13th century. **Den gamle Farvergård** (the Old Dyeworks), with shop and dyehouse, has also been converted into a museum. In contrast, the **Glass Museum**, in the former Custom House, shows modern pieces made by over 400 international glass-makers, and demonstrations are given in summer.

On the coast are three harbours – for fishing, for yachts and for trade – and also a ferry service to Zealand (1 hour 40 minutes to Sjællands Odde). The major coastal attraction is the *Jylland*, the world's largest wooden ship, launched in 1860 and currently being restored. An unusual feature is the sea-based **Windmill Park**: the windmills generate enough energy to supply about 600 houses.

The beaches in **Ebeltoft Bay** are safe, sandy and clean. The area is suitable for windsurfing and fishing.

Fishing boats at Esbjerg are painted the traditional pastel blue

Accommodation

Several hotels have apartments or bungalows, in which you must stay for at least a week. Such is the central **Hotel Vigen** (tel: 86 34 48 00). The larger and dearer **Hvide Hus** (tel: 86 34 14 66) and **Ebeltoft Strand** (tel: 86 34 33 00) both overlook the sea. All have indoor pools. Near the Windmill Park is **Ebeltoft Maritime Ferieby Øer**, a holiday village of 300 bungalows, with a sports hall, swimming pool, marina, shops and restaurants.

Restaurants

Two restaurants in the main street specialise in Danish food: the elegant **Ane Kirstine** and **Mellem Jyder**, in a half-timbered building with a garden.

ESBJERG

The ice-free port of Esbjerg is the largest and most modern fishing port in Scandinavia. Britons coming to Denmark with their cars land at Esbjerg, and although there may be a strong whiff of fish near the fish factory if the wind blows onshore, a couple of museums and the large shopping centre are worth visiting.

Esbjerg is a comparatively new town, built around the turn of the century in the so-called 'American' period, designed on a grid pattern with a motley collection of towers and spires. Visitors can take a motorboat tour (summer only) of the fishing and commercial harbours, leaving from the Fanø ferry berth.

Sightseeing

The Danish fishing industry and its history is well documented at the new Fiskeri-og Søfartsmuseet (Fisheries and Maritime Museum), two miles (3km) north of the town. The museum has rescued and refitted several types of old fishing boats, and different types of line and net fishing, the routes of the eel trade and the demise of the cutter are explained in an enthralling way. Outside, various boats, shipwrecks and old fishermen's huts are now displayed amongst specially created sand dunes. A harbour and shipyard are being built. The museum also has a saltwater aquarium and a Sealarium.

In the **Esbjerg Museum**, buildings in the town have been constructed to form streets as they were from 1900–40, and a second exhibition showing the town's earliest history has just been completed. **Esbjerg Kunstforenings Samling** (Modern Art Museum) is devoted to Danish artists from 1920 to the present. At the Fanø ferry harbour the old lightship, *Horns Rev*, can be visited.

Accommodation

The centrally located **Britannia** (tel: 75 13 01 11) is modern and reasonably priced. The Hermitage Hotel West (tel: 75 13 55 00), on American motel lines, is set in a deer park 2 miles (3km) from the centre. A cheaper hotel in town is the **Park Hotel** (tel: 75 12 08 68), and there are special prices for children sharing their parents' room.

Restaurants

Good value food is available at **Restaurant Bourgogne** on Skolegade and **Restaurant Kunstpavillonen** (Havnegåde 20), in the Art Museum building (tel: 75 12 64 95). **Sand's Restaurant** is the oldest in Esbjerg (Skolegade 60), and **Café Danmark** is traditionally furnished.

Entertainment

Skolegåde is the best street for discos. **Bonbonnieren** has a restaurant and a disco, while **Sams Bar** is a discos which sells beer. **5 Eiffel** on Englandsgåde is a jazz restaurant. **You'll Never Walk Alone** is a real English pub, Kongensgade 10.

Excursions from Esbjerg

About seven miles (12km) north of Esbjerg is the **Marbæk Nature Park**, where marked paths lead to scenic routes by sand dunes, cliffs and forests.

◆
FYRKAT

This is the smallest of Denmark's Viking forts (see box), thought to have been built around AD980 and used for about 20 years. Made of wood and stacked turves, the fort had dry moats on two sides, and four gateways. The ramparts and ring fort have been recreated and the post holes filled in to outline the former position of streets and houses. Inside the circular rampart were 16 houses, in groups of four round a courtyard. A similar three-room wooden Viking longhouse has been built outside the ramparts, its roof covered with oak chips. About 50 people would have lived here, sleeping on low benches along the walls. There is a central fireplace and it is thought that the smoke dispersed through louvres in the gables. There is evidence that the buildings were destroyed in a fire after the inhabitants had left.

A new 'Viking' settlement of nine houses will illustrate the living conditions of the Viking peasant.

Outside the fort is a small burial ground where skeletons of women and children have been found, some accompanied by gifts they were taking to the next world. Finds from the site are on view at the **Hobro Museum**. 'Viking' activities take place in summer and a Viking play is performed.

Viking Forts

It is thought that the Danish king Harald Bluetooth ordered the defences at Fyrkat to be built. The structural accuracy of this site – exactly 120 metres (about 394ft) in diameter, and equal spacing between the houses – shows a high level of technical skills. The Vikings' four Danish strongholds, at Trelleborg, Aggersborg, Nonnebakken and Fyrkat were all military centres, and were probably bases for westward expeditions. At Fyrkat, few weapons have been found, but spindles and warps, goldsmiths' melting pots and items of jewellery indicate that the Vikings also led a peaceful domestic existence.

◆◆
GAMMEL ESTRUP
Jyllands Herregårdsmuseum
(Jutland Manor House Museum)
and **Dansk Landbrugsmuseum**
(Danish Agricultural Museum)
are two good reasons for
visiting this attractive part of
rural Djursland. Gammel Estrup
is near the village of Auning, on
the road between Grenå and
Randers.

The Manor House is a fine,
moated Renaissance castle and
the earliest part was built
towards the end of the 15th
century. It was inhabited by two
noble families, once political
advisors to the Danish royal
family. Their descendants
founded the museum, which
contains their heirlooms and
family portraits.

Its rooms are elegant, with
painted ceilings, French and
English furniture and porcelain.
A 17th-century turret wall has
been plastered to imitate
drapery.

The Agricultural Museum is in a
separate building in the

Replica Viking longhouse at Fyrkat

grounds. It was founded over a
century ago and houses a
collection of over 25,000
agricultural implements. A
permanent exhibition of farm
interiors illustrates two
centuries of Danish country life.
In summer children can try out
for themselves old farming
methods such as threshing with
flail or grinding corn, and the
local Guild of Blacksmiths gives
demonstrations.

There are pleasant gardens
and a café. Energetic visitors
can hire a canoe from Sjellebro
by contacting the tourist office
at Auning (tel: 86 48 34 44).

◆
HERNING
This modern town is the centre
of the Danish textile industry
and hosts international trade
fairs at its exhibition complex. It
also has some good museums
and outstanding art collections
and is popular with anglers for
its sea trout.

JUTLAND

Sightseeing

The **Herning Museum** is not particularly noteworthy, but next door is **Danmarks Fotomuseum** (Photographic Museum), where changing exhibitions of Danish and foreign photographers are held. There is a huge panoramic photograph of Copenhagen and a fine collection of holographs and old cameras.

More memorable are the modern art collections one mile (2km) east of the town. At the circular **Carl-Henning Pedersen and Else Alfelt's Museum** are over 4,000 works of art by this couple, and 100 yards (90m) of outside walls are covered with brightly coloured ceramic slabs. Close by, the **Herning Kunstmuseum** (Art Museum) and a sculpture park with works dating from the 1950s, both circular, contain works by international and Danish artists. Beyond are **De Geometriske Haver** (the Geometrical Gardens).

The town's oldest building, the imposing manor house of **Herningsholm** (1579), is now a museum for the poet Steen Steensen Blicher (1782–1848). The house has been fully restored and the painted ceilings and murals show to advantage the poet's manuscripts and memorabilia. Visitors can also see paintings of the Jutland landscape and an unusual collection of Danish country scenes of the 1920s which are set in small boxes, a type of three-dimensional diorama, or peepshow, created by Inge Faurtoft.

KOLDING

In 1268 **Koldinghus Castle** was built on a rocky bluff by the Danish King Erik V as a fortress against the Duchy of Schleswig. Later monarchs added towers and chapels and rebuilt the fortress as a castle. After a chequered history of fire, military occupation and abandonment, the castle was rebuilt in 1890. Today **Museet på Koldinghus** is a lakeside museum, the oldest part dating from the 15th century.

A visit to this red brick castle provides good exercise, for access from one wing to another is often only possible by descending to the courtyard and climbing up again. The museum is crammed with Gothic and Romanesque church sculpture, heavy oak furniture, relics from the Schleswig Wars, Chinese porcelain, European pictures and interiors dating from the 16th century onwards.

In the impressive Ruin Hall, original brick pillars are protected under a light roof, supported by new wooden pillars and linked to a high-tech gallery to recreate the original lofty dimensions. The castle church is home to a colony of Pipistrelle bats.

Other sights in Kolding include the old timbered pharmacy, **Borchs Gård** and the later neo-Romanesque town hall.

Kunstmuseet Trapholt is a new museum of modern art in a park, showing expressionism, abstract art, design (in ceramics and textiles) and furniture by Danish artists. **Den**

The ancient fortress of Koldinghus

Geografiske Have (the Geographical Garden), south-east of Kolding, is a pleasant haven – a huge garden with over 2,000 shrubs and trees, glasshouses and Europe's longest bamboo hedge.

Accommodation

Surrounded by woodland, **Hotel Koldingfjord** (tel: 75 51 00 00) occupies an enviable position on the fjord shore. Just as expensive but closer to town is the modern **Hotel Scanticon** (tel: 75 50 15 55). Cheaper and more central is **Hotel Kolding** (tel: 75 52 50 00), with the popular basement **Café Baxx**.

Restaurants

Restaurant Tre Roser (tel: 75 53 21 22) at the edge of the park (Byparken) serves good food, including game. **Den Gyldne Hane** (tel: 75 52 97 20), in a traditional building near the Geographical Garden, offers a comprehensive menu. The harbourside **Restaurant Admiralen** (tel: 75 52 04 21) specialises in seafood.

Entertainment

Kridthuset Jazz Club has live music at weekends.

LEGOLAND ✓

Billund

There cannot be many children (or adults, for that matter) who have not grown up with a box of Lego bricks and here, in the town of Billund where they are made, is Legoland – a unique theme park which combines thrilling rides with enormous Lego models.

Outdoor Miniland is probably the best known feature, with its

Youngsters hit the road in Legoland

JUTLAND

scale model towns and villages including Lego versions of Amalienborg square, a pretty Rhineland scene and an airport – truly an inspiration to modellers everywhere.

Fabuland is where the rides are, although it has to be said that teenagers would find them a bit tame. This is a park for younger children, who seem to particularly enjoy the Traffic School with its brightly-coloured electric cars and authentic road layouts (staff are

It all works, from boats to bridges

Mount Rushmore in miniature

on hand to make sure they stick to the rules of the road).

Legoredo Town, dominated by a huge model of the Monument of the Presidents on Mount Rushmore, takes visitors to the American West. Here they can pan for gold in the **Legoldmine** or cook over an open campfire in the company of a friendly Indian.

You can get your bearings of the park by taking a trip on the monorail or miniature train, or by going up the observation tower.

Indoor exhibits include the magnificent Titania's Palace containing around 3,000 priceless miniatures, antique dolls and dolls' houses, mechanical toys, Lego World Show and a children's playroom with thousands of Lego bricks.

Legoland is open from Easter to mid-December; open-air attractions are only open from May to mid-September.

◆
LIMFJORD

The Limfjord area is an extensive landscape of inland waters formed by Ice Age glaciers, its many lakes and rivers providing a sanctuary for birds. Much of the west coast has silted up and part of it is now protected by dikes. The western (Thy) area is flat with a mixture of woods, bog and sand dunes; the east is hillier, with moors. This varied landscape, with wide, clean beaches makes it specially attractive for outdoor types. Interesting places to visit include prehistoric remains, museums, amusement parks, churches and manor houses.

Sightseeing

Hjerl Hede, near Vinderup, is the rural setting of **Den Gamle Landsby** (the Old Village), with many old buildings, such as farmhouses, a forge and a dairy attractively arranged round a large pond, to show how the Danish village has developed since 1500. From mid-June to mid-August the village comes to life as corn is milled, bread baked and pots fired by people dressed in period costume. Grazing sheep and cattle complete the scene. In a 'Stone Age' settlement flint implements and dugout canoes are made. Mors is connected to the mainland by four bridges, and technically no longer an island. The south is flat with salt marshes, but the north is hillier, ending with coastal cliffs. Fine sandy beaches in the west are backed by pine trees. The **Molermuseum** near Sejerslev

displays fossils and diatomites; more are on the beaches at Hanklit and Feggeklit (where it is alleged Hamlet killed his stepfather).

In Scandinavia's largest flower park, **Jesperhus Blomsterpark**, to the south of Nykøbing, half a million flowers bloom. Palms and tropical plants, fountains and waterfalls, birds butterflies, snakes and crocodiles make for an exciting day out.

Spøttrup, near Rødding, is a beautifully preserved 15th-century fortress built for the Viborg bishops. It has a double moat and its ramparts are 25ft (9m) high. The kitchens, dungeons, narrow staircases and the Great Hall instantly evoke the spirit and hardships (note the toilet facilities!) of those times. The attractive Renaissance garden contains herbs and medicinal plants. Thisted is the charming main town on Thy, a peninsula between the North Sea and the Limfjord, with a Gothic-style church. The **Thisted Museum**, in a private mansion, has a well displayed collection. Prize exhibits are five gold Bronze Age boats. Later objects include ceramics, glass, buckles, old shop signs, historic house interiors and regional costumes.

At **Vestervig** is the largest village church in Scandinavia. The white building, once part of a 12th-century monastery, is visible from more than two miles (4km) away. Inside are high arched vaults, painted pews and pulpit, a starry fresco and several Romanesque tombstones.

Accommodation

At Thisted the comfortable **Hotel Aalborg** (tel: 97 92 35 66) overlooks the harbour and the central **Hotel Thisted** (tel: 97 92 52 00) has good food. Larger and more modern, **Hotel Limfjorden** (tel: 97 92 40 11) overlooks the fjord. In Nykøbing, **Pakhuset** (tel: 97 72 33 00) has a good reputation; the charming old **Sallingsund Færgekro** (tel: 97 72 00 88) by the fjord offers a traditional atmosphere and food.

◆◆
MARIAGER

This is a charming village – often called the town of roses because they flourish here – of cobbled streets, lined with small corn-coloured, half-timbered houses. The **museum**, located in an 18th-century merchant's house, has an unusual external gallery and contains a good collection from the Stone Age, Bronze Age implements, and later domestic utensils. A peasant's room is furnished in the style of 1700, and the museum's founder donated a rococo room.

The 15th-century **church**, built as part of a nunnery, is a large white building set on a hill surrounded by mature trees and an immaculate graveyard. It is worth going inside to see the painted pulpit, galleries, and one surviving fresco.

In complete contrast, the yacht harbour on the fjord is a lively place.

The **Mariager–Handest Vintage Railway** runs daily in July, Sundays only in June and August.

◆
MARIAGER FJORD

This is the longest fjord in Denmark, and Hobro is the narrowest place where it can be bridged. Hobro has a museum in the old grocer's shop, with finds from Fyrkat. The new **Ibsens Samling af Nyere Kunst** (Ibsen Collection of Recent Art) is housed in a building overlooking the fjord. The fjord scenery is pretty and the Bramslev Bakker (hills) to the north offer a fine viewpoint.

Accommodation

In Hobro, the **Hotel Alpina** (tel: 98 52 28 00) and the **Motel Hobro** (tel: 98 52 28 88) are both very comfortable. For a stay in a traditional half-timbered building, sensitively restored and well furnished, the **Hotel Postgården** (tel: 98 54 10 12) near Mariager marketplace is ideal. **Motel Landgangen** (tel: 98 54 11 22) has views across the fjord. The **Hotel Hadsund** (tel: 98 57 42 55) has also been refurbished and is located in woods. In the countryside between Mariager and Randers, the 300-year old **Hvidsten Kro** (see below) has a good reputation.

Restaurants

Hvidsten Kro (tel: 86 47 70 22) in Spentrup serves salt herring and Swedish herrings in its historic saloon, and the cliff-top restaurant at **Bramslev Bakker** near Hobro (tel: 98 52 52 00) welcomes families. The two hotels in Mariager also do good meals. In Hobro, the **Traktørstedet** and **Spisestedet** restaurants are good value.

Old timbered cottage at Mariager

◆◆
RIBE

In the flat and flood-prone marshlands of southern Denmark, where storks build their nests each spring, stands the medieval town of Ribe, now safely enclosed by the river (Ribe Å) and a ring road. This is Denmark's oldest town, with over 500 preserved buildings lining its cobbled streets. The Vikings first developed Ribe as a commercial centre, transporting their goods by river. A wooden church was built here in AD860, and 100 years later a bishopric was established. Ribe became Denmark's most important trading town because of the convergence of sea trade routes. After the Reformation however, its fortunes waned as the river silted up and the population decreased.

Sightseeing

The cathedral is one of Denmark's oldest surviving buildings: parts of the present church were built in about 1150. The lofty interior is mostly Romanesque and the walls are adorned with sepulchral monuments of local and national notables. The red brick tower was built around 1300 (after an earlier one collapsed) to warn the inhabitants of impending disasters.

Two bishop's residences survive from the 15th and 16th centuries: **Puggård,** now part of the cathedral school, and **Hans Tusens Hus,** now a museum with many Viking finds.

Many houses in the town are half-timbered, with attractive doors and richly carved frames. A small museum has been created inside the former debtors' prison in the town hall, recalling civic history with spiked maces and an executioner's axe.

Sct Catharinae Kirke og Kloster (St Catherine's Church and Abbey) were founded by Dominican monks. **Quedens Gård,** a 16th-century merchant's house, is now a fascinating museum of interiors from 1580.

Accommodation

Accommodation in Ribe is limited. Two old (16th-century) and pretty hotels on the main square, furnished with antiques, are the **Dagmar** (tel: 75 42 00 33) and the **Weis Stue** (tel: 75 42 07 00). Both have atmospheric cellar restaurants. The nightwatchman starts his rounds from here at 22.30hrs.

Excursions from Ribe

Two water trips are worth taking: one from the city harbour at Skibbroen through the marshes to the **Kammersluse** (sluice); the second via the ebb road to the tiny island of **Mandø**, a bird and seal sanctuary.

◆

REBILD HILLS

Rebild Bakker (Hills), rising to a height of only 318ft (116m) above sea level, were formed during the Ice Age and are now covered with aspen, juniper and beech. Much of the heathland was bought in 1912 by Danish Americans who donated it to Denmark as a national park. Now thousands of people flock to the Rebild Festival each year on US Independence day, 4 July. The **Lincoln Log Cabin Museum** at Rebild illustrates the story of the early Danish pioneers to the US and the conditions in which they lived.

South of the park is **Rold Skov** (Rold Forest), Denmark's largest wooded area and the only remaining fragment of the forest which once covered Himmerland. In addition to beech, oak and conifers there are bogs, meadows, springs and lakes. The largest lake is Madum Sø; a stroll round Store Økssø, the second largest lake, takes about an hour. In **Troldeskov** (Troll Forest) is a weird collection of gnarled beech trees.

The Lindeborg River flows underground along the western edge of the forest and several springs rise here, bringing down huge quantities of water of a constant volume and temperature 45–46°F (7–8°C). The largest is Lille Blåkilde (Little Blue Spring) which produces 33 gallons (150 litres) per second.

Other sights of interest include burial mounds and dolmen (off Buderupholmvej, northeast of the national park), and **Den Jyske Skovhave** (Jutland Arboretum). In Skørping the church has good frescos, and the **Spillemandsmuseet** (Folk Music Museum) has sections on hunting, handicrafts and regional culture.

Rebild and Støvring are good starting points to explore this area. The tourist offices publish maps with suggested driving, cycling and walking routes. Walkers and cyclists without maps can follow marked paths

Accommodation and Restaurants

Skørping has two comfortable hotels with good food: **Rold Stor Kro** (tel: 98 37 51 00) and **Hotel Rebild Park** (tel: 98 39 14 00). North of Rebild, at Stovring, is **Støvring Kro** (tel: 98 37 13 22), a traditional inn with a good reputation and cellar. **Rebildhus** serves food only, and has fine park views.

◆◆
SILKEBORG

This is the main town in Denmark's lake district, a pretty area with about a dozen lakes, some interconnected by Denmark's longest river, the Gudenå. Much of the land is wooded, and several nature trails weave round lakes or along the river valley.

The highest hill is the 482ft (147m) **Himmelbjerget** (active visitors can walk up to an observation tower), best visited on the 130-year old paddle steamer *Hjejlen*, which sails regularly from Silkeborg. You can disembark at intermediate landing stages, take a walk, and pick up a later boat.

Silkeborg is a fairly new town, established in 1846 when barges were the sole means of transport and Michael Drewsen, a local merchant, founded a water-powered paper mill. Paper-making is still one of the town's most important industries, and Drewsen's comfortable living room has been transplanted to the **Silkeborg Museum**.

The museum is the resting place of the 'Tollund Man', preserved in a peat bog since 220BC, and found in 1950. He is now chief exhibit in the museum's new wing devoted to the Iron Age, and wears a worried frown beneath his pointed sheepskin cap. He met his death by hanging, possibly as a sacrifice to the gods. Life-size models of Iron Age women clearly show their complicated hairstyles and contemporary fashions. Methods of agriculture and iron-ore extraction are also

Denmark's beautiful lake district

shown. The older museum building contains items of local historic interest, including glass and workshops. In the garden is a wooden Iron Age dwelling with wattle walls.

The **Silkeborg Art Museum** contains a collection of modern European art mainly by members of the COBRA group (from Copenhagen, Brussels and Amsterdam). The group was founded by Asger Jorn whose watercolours, oils and ceramics are also displayed here.

Accommodation and Restaurants

Two fairly expensive hotels under the same management are the comfortable **Hotel Dania** (tel: 86 82 01 11) in the main square, and **Hotel Himmelbjerget** (tel: 86 89 80 45). A bigger, modern hotel outside town is the **Impala** (tel: 86 82 03 00), with a lake view. About five miles (8km) north-east of Silkeborg is **Svostrup Kro** (tel: 86 87 70 04), in an attractive country setting. Two good places to eat are **Godt Gemt** in the town square, and **Piaf Kafe** along Nygade.

◆◆◆
SKAGEN ✓

There are few places in Europe where two seas meet, but the north of Denmark is one of them. Small-scale maps show Skagen as the northernmost point, but it is actually Grenen. Here, the waves of the Kattegat and Skaggerrak crash against each other, and strong winds and fierce waves make this a dramatic and dangerous spot. A walk across the sand (how long a walk depends on whether the tides are in or out) or a ride in a tractor-bus will take you to a notice forbidding bathing. Between the car park and the Skaw is the stone slab commemorating the poet and painter Holger Drachmann, who lived in Skagen.

Skagen is divided into two parts – Gammel Skagen (old Skagen, usually abbreviated to Gl Skagen) on the Skaggerak side, and Skagen on the Kattegat. Gl Skagen has a wide, sandy beach and consists mainly of hotels and painted yellow houses, many of which are owned on a time-share basis.

Sightseeing

The town became an artists' colony in the 1870s because of the unusual quality of the northern light. The painters used to meet in the dining room of Brøndums Hotel, and paint each other's portraits; these now hang on the wood-panelled walls, and this entire room has been incorporated into the purpose-built **Skagen Museum**, where pictures they, and other artists, painted between 1870 and 1930 are beautifully displayed.

The best known of the Skagen artists are P S Krøyer, Michael and Anna Ancher (she was the daughter of the owner of Brøndums Hotel) and Laurits Tuxen. Themes in the Skagen Museum reflect local life and

Sea defences on the Skagen shore

include seascapes, fishermen, rural scenes and seaside pictures of the artists themselves.

A few minutes walk away is **Michael og Anna Anchers Hus** (the Anchers' House) where they lived from 1884, and which has been faithfully restored. Their furniture and personal belongings bring the museum to life and pictures – mostly theirs – completely cover the walls. Next door is **Saxilds Gård** (entry with the same ticket), an unfurnished villa hung with early sketches and completed paintings which, until now, have never been on display. **Drachmanns Hus**, called Villa Pax, has also been restored and contains paintings by Drachmann and his friends, as well as his sketchbooks and manuscripts.

Skagen Fortidsminder (Open-Air Museum) comprises half a dozen buildings and a windmill. It is mostly devoted to fishing, on which the town's livelihood has depended for over 200 years (a large port, fish packing and processing plant survive to this day), and includes reminders of the constant dangers faced at sea.

Den Tilsandede Kirke was a large rural church built at the end of the 14th century and dedicated to Sct Laurentii (St Laurence), patron saint of seafarers. The dire effects of wind and sand not only ruined the surrounding farmland but also engulfed the church. After a huge storm in 1775 the congregation had to dig their way in, and 20 years later the church was closed. Now all that

remains is the white step-gabled tower.

Accommodation
Brøndums Hotel (tel: 98 44 15 55), by the museum, is full of character and the dining room has paintings by the Skagen artists. Two new hotels, the more centrally located **Skagen Motel** (tel: 98 44 45 35) and the costlier **Hotel Skagen** (tel: 98 44 22 33), with an outdoor pool, both lie northwest of the town. In Gl Skagen are two good seaside hotels, **Hotel Højengran** (tel: 98 44 22 58) and **Strandhotellet** (tel: 98 44 56 57).

♦♦
TØNDER

Situated in the flat, marshy land of southwest Denmark near the German border, Tønder, one of Denmark's oldest towns, is a charming collection of well-preserved gabled houses and cobbled streets. Tønder was an important port, mainly shipping cattle, trading with towns in northern Germany and the Netherlands and frequently changing allegiance between Denmark and Germany. When the North Sea began to encroach in the 1550s dikes were built, but the town was badly flooded at least twice over the next 300 years. For a while lacemaking became the main occupation, but although some still carry on the craft, lacemaking eventually declined and cattle trading re-emerged. Many of the fine old Renaissance-style houses were built by lace merchants, their bow windows providing more light for the workers.

Sightseeing

The richly decorated **Kristkirken** (Christ Church), built in 1592, has a rood screen bearing religious portraits, ornate epitaphs and a singers' gallery.

The town has two museums. The **Tønder Museum** in the gatehouse of the 16th-century castle contains objects illuminating the town's past – Dutch and Friesian wall tiles, table silver, locally made furniture and lace.

Sønderjyllands Kunstmuseum (South Jutland Museum of Art) holds a large collection of works by 19th- and 20th-century Danish sculptors and artists, and surrealist pictures from northern Europe. **Det gamle Apotek** (the Old Pharmacy) is still prominent and holds exhibitions; the thick-walled basement is 400 years old. The annual folk music festival takes place at the end of August.

Accommodation and Restaurants

In town, **Hostrups Hotel** (tel: 74 72 21 29) is comfortable, with a river view and garden courtyard. **Longhorn Restaurant** (Vestergåde 85) is worth a try. **Stigs Restaurant**, at Sdr KLandeveg 3, and **Christies**, at Ribe Landeveg 37, are both excellent. In Møgel-tønder, **Schackenborg Slotskro** is a restaurant in a castle wing.

Excursions from Tønder

Three miles (5km) west of Tønder is **Møgeltønder**, whose main street, Slotsgåde, is often called the most beautiful village street in Denmark. With its shady lime trees, cobblestones and old thatched houses, it runs between Schackenborg Castle (now owned by Prince Joachim, the Queen's younger son) and the church. This is the town's oldest building, the nave dating from 1275. The lovely and unusual interior, with coloured murals and a frieze, mostly dates from the 16th century. The gold altarpiece is framed by a triumphal arch, and a balcony decorated with religious portraits leads to the pew of the former Count Schack.

Just 10 miles (17km) north of Tønder, **Løgumkloster** is famous for its large abbey church, and one remaining wing of a 12th-century monastery. Close by is a 68ft (25m) high carillon, with 49 bells, the biggest in Scandinavia, presented to the town in 1973 on its 800th annniversary.

◆

VEJLE

Vejle is both a thriving port and a holiday centre. It exports a wide range of goods from textiles to chewing gum, and is also the home of Denmark's largest sausage factory.

Vejle is attractively set amid the wooded slopes of Norreskøv in the north and Munkebjerg to the south.

Sightseeing

The town is hilly, with old winding lanes and a very long traffic-free street. Gothic **Sct Nikolai Kirke** (St Nicholas Church) is the oldest building, and contains the glass-lidded coffin of a woman from about

This windmill at Skagen is thatched

500BC, discovered in a nearby peatbog during the last century. On the first floor of the half-timbered building which houses the Tourist Office is an interesting local exhibition, including finds from Viking tombs and domestic utensils buried during the war with Sweden. The old **Mill** on Koldingvej is a landmark worth visiting. **Vejle Museum** displays local archaeological finds, and nextdoor is **Vejle Kunstmuseum** (Art Museum), with one of Denmark's best modern collections of graphics, paintings and sculptures.

Accommodation

The **Munkebjerg Hotel** (tel: 75 72 35 00), four miles (6km) outside the town, is big and expensive, with extensive grounds and a casino. In town are the reasonably priced and comfortable **Hotel Vejle** (tel: 75 82 32 11) and the cosy family **Park Hotel** (tel: 75 82 24 66).

Restaurants

Jensens Bøfhus and the newer **A Centret** are both good, the former specialising in beef, the latter in Danish food.

Excursions from Vejle

On the southern side of the fjord, there are sandy beaches at Andkær Vig bay and around Hvidbjerg/Mørkholt with its extensive dunes.

Jelling is well worth seeing, and has some amazing monuments marking important events in Danish history. Two large mounds in the village centre are thought to be the burial places of the Viking King Gorm and his Queen, Thyra, who died around AD935. Outside the white-washed church are two rune stones erected as monuments to them. The **Great Rune Stone**, erected by their son, Harald Bluetooth, has been called Denmark's baptismal certificate as its inscriptions recall Denmark's unification, its adoption of Christianity and the conquest of Norway. The church, on the site of a much larger wooden one built by Harald, contains old frescos, a chambered tomb and various ornaments thought to have belonged to King Gorm. Legend has it that Harald reburied his pagan father in the church after his (Harald's) conversion to Christianity. **Randbøl Hede** (Moor) is another pretty place to visit. History buffs should see **Ravning Bridge** (1,000 years old), the **Egtved Girl's Grave** (her body is in the National Museum) and the **Old Military Road**. This is the old medieval military and trade route (*Hærvejen*) which ran between Jutland and Schleswig Holstein in Germany.

◆

VIBORG

Viborg can trace its history back to the eighth century when pagans worshipped here; later the advent of Christianity brought a cathedral (AD1130) and a bishop's see, and Danish kings were crowned here until 1665.

The town sits astride two lakes and its location in the centre of Jutland made it an important trading centre. Much of the original architecture was destroyed in two great fires, in 1567 and 1726. Today it is a market town, with a small historic centre and some fine old houses, especially along Sct Mogensgåde.

Sightseeing

Viborg is dominated by its twin towered **cathedral**, but only the crypt survives from the original building. The rest was rebuilt during the last century in Romanesque style. The most striking interior features are richly-coloured murals of biblical scenes, by Joakim Skovgaard, who also painted the ceilings. A quiet public

garden outside the west door, **Latinerhaven** (Latin Garden), once belonged to the Latin master at the cathedral school. In the old town hall is the **Skovgaard Museum** exhibiting a variety of craftwork – silver, furniture, bookbinding, paintings – by three generations of the Skovgaard family and their friends. Joakim's sketchbooks with preliminary drawings for the cathedral are included. The **Stiftsmuseum** (District Museum) in Hjultorvet portrays the town's history in thematic displays such as craft workshops.

Accommodation and Restaurants

The **Golf Hotel Viborg** (tel: 86 61 02 22) is a long, low building in a beautiful lakeside setting. Five miles (8km) southeast is **Rindsholm Kro** (tel: 86 63 90 44), a small comfortable inn renowned for its good food, with an old garden.

Two good restaurants in Viborg are in Sct Mathias Gade: **Ly** (no 78) and **Messing Jens** (no 48).

Excursions from Viborg

West of Viborg are two fascinating limestone mines (*kalkgruber*). The **Mønsted mines** were worked for 1,000 years and are the largest in Denmark, with 25 miles (40km) of galleries, up to 65 feet (20m) high, which now provide a cool home for thousands of bats. There are also limestone and bat museums here, cheese storage (about 200 tons of it!) and the occasional classical concert. **Daugbjerg** is older, smaller and darker.

◆
AALBORG (ÅLBORG)

This modern, vibrant city is the fourth largest in Denmark and lies on the southern bank of the Limfjord. Its wealth is now based on the manufacture of cement and aquavit, no longer on herring and tobacco. Aalborg can trace its history back to the Vikings, and in 1992 celebrated 1,300 years since they first settled nearby. Much of the town has been rebuilt since the war, but although tall glass and concrete structures now dwarf the clusters of older buildings, there are still some attractive areas with fine 17th-century and half-timbered houses, some relocated from other streets (the junction at Nørregade and Fjordgade is a particularly good example).

Aa-h!
In the Danish alphabet, aa is replaced by å. However, the town of Aalborg prefers to keep this spelling. In an alphabetical listing of towns, you will still find it at the end, after Z, along with all the Ås.

Sightseeing

Jens Bangs Stenhus, at Østerå 9, is an ornate five-storey brick house with unusual curved gables, built in 1624 by a local merchant, Jens Bang. It is claimed to be Scandinavia's largest private house from the Renaissance, and stands close to the baroque Rådhus (Town Hall), built around 1760. The gargoyles are said to represent councillors of Bang's day who would not elect him. Today the

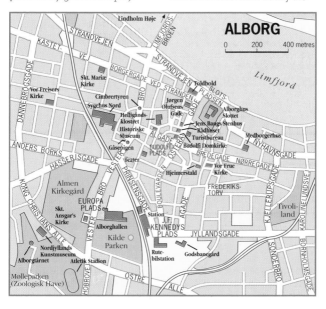

Gargoyle at Jen Bangs Stenhus

building is a pharmacy (as it has been for 300 years), and the vaulted cellar is a popular wine bar.

Vestiges of earlier occupation can be seen in the **Aalborg Historiske Museum** (Historical Museum), which displays many items dating from the Stone Age. One of its treasures is the 1602 Aalborg Room, removed from a merchant's home and reconstructed here. Panelled in richly carved oak with a frieze of biblical quotations, it has a coffered ceiling. The museum also has a good collection of glass.

Budolfi Domkirke (St Botolphs Cathedral) is a whitewashed brick edifice in Gothic style, built around 1400, with a later baroque spire. Inside it has a carved pulpit, large altarpiece and some early frescos.

Helligåndsklostret (the Monastery of the Holy Ghost) is a redbrick, step-gabled building almost the same age as Budolfi. A former nunnery and monastery, it was dedicated to the care of the ill and elderly, work which continues today. It is Denmark's oldest social institution (1431) and visitors can go on conducted tours to see the monks' refectory and the 16th-century frescos on the chapel ceiling.

Aalborghus Slot (Castle) is a white, step-gabled building near the harbour. Built in the 16th century as a fortress by King Christian III, it never served this purpose but instead became the residence of the king's representative. Now visitors can tour the dungeons, casemates and ramparts.

Aalborg Søfarts- og Marinemuseum (Shipping and Naval Museum) is brand new. Sited near the west end of the harbour area, it shows the development of civil and military shipping in Denmark, particularly during the last 200 years. Denmark's last submarine, *Springeren*, has been installed on dry land and a section is devoted to Aalborg's own shipbuilding industry.

Nordjyllands Kunstmuseum (Museum of Fine Art) is an outstanding modern building designed by Finnish architects Elissa and Alvar Aalto, with Danish architect Jean-Jaques Baruël, built 1968–1972 and set in a large woodland area. The museum has a permanent collection of Danish and foreign art dating from the end of the last century, and a children's museum. The sculpture park is dominated by the glass pyramid ('Dream Palace') by Bjørn Nørgaard, and an amphitheatre where music and variety shows are staged.

Close by is **Aalborgtårnet** (Aalborg Tower), 344ft (105m) above sea level, which gives a fine view of the town and the fjord (there is a lift).

Other attractions are the **Zoologisk Have** (Zoo) in Mølleparken, **Vandland**, a large tropical water park, and **Tivoliland**, within walking distance of the town centre.

Transport

City sightseeing tours (with English commentary) lasting over two hours start from Adelgåde on summer weekdays at 11.00hrs. If you want to travel around on your own, buy a two-day Aalborg Pass (*Pas*), which gives free city bus travel and free or reduced entry to museums and other attractions. The passes can be bought from hotels, museums and from the tourist office.

Accommodation

For a central hotel try the new **Chagall** (tel: 98 12 69 33), or the **Slotshotellet** near the waterfront (tel: 98 10 14 00). In a parkland setting is the recently renovated **Hotel Hvide Hus** (tel: 98 13 84 00), with a 15th-floor restaurant. The **Park Hotel** (tel: 98 12 31 33) near the station is cheaper, and its restaurant is decorated with original works of art.

Restaurants

There are over 300 restaurants in Aalborg. Jomfru Ane Gade is a pretty and popular pedestrian-only street, with Denmark's longest continuous stretch of pubs and restaurants. **Cafeen og Dufy** at no 8 is situated in an old house, and upstairs is the smarter **Restaurant Dufy**. At no 21 is **Restaurant Faklen** with an intimate atmosphere. For fish, try the more expensive **Penny Lane Fish Restaurant**, at Sankelmarksgade 9.

Entertainment

Aalborg is second only to Copenhagen for its nightlife. Many restaurants and pubs offer jazz, rock and folk music, as well as dancing, billiards and dice. For serious entertainment, the modern **Aalborg Hall** has its own symphony orchestra, and visiting theatre groups also perform there. The **Aalborg Theatre** stages productions in Danish.

Excursions from Aalborg

Lindholm Høje lies north of Limfjord, which separates Aalborg from Nørresundby. It is a Viking burial ground with 682 graves, in which cremated bodies were interred together with burial objects. A recent museum on the site shows living conditions in Viking times.

◆◆◆
ÅRHUS ✓

Århus, on Jutland's east coast, is Denmark's second largest city, with some well-designed modern buildings and a cluster of old ones around the cathedral. The city is enhanced by lots of green space. Culture thrives: there are about a dozen museums, several small theatres and an exciting modern concert hall. The university and other educational institutions support a large young population (currently 30,000) and the music scene – rock and the city's annual festival in September – is the brightest in Denmark.

Århus's valley situation and proximity to the sea caused the Vikings to settle here a thousand years ago. As a trading centre the town flourished, but in the Middle

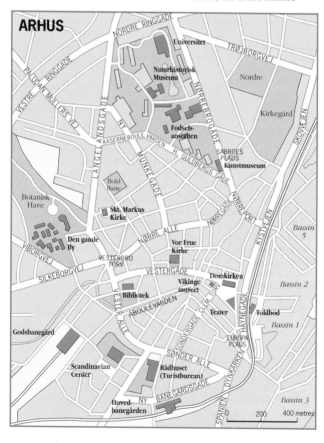

Ages the population fell dramatically as a result of wars and the Black Death. Later, the city prospered again and today Århus has the largest container terminal in Denmark – food processing is the most important industry.

Sightseeing

Domkirken (the cathedral) is Denmark's longest church. Originally a Romanesque basilica built in 1200, it was destroyed by fire and rebuilt in Gothic style in the late 15th century. Note the vault by the pre-Reformation Lübeck master craftsman Bernt Notke, and the modern, painted glass window by the Norwegian Emmanuel Vigeland.

Viking remains found near the cathedral show that this part of the city has always been the centre of the Århus community. The old walls which surrounded the Viking town, a typical dwelling and tools can all be seen at the site of the excavation, in the basement of Unibank, at Clemens Torv, now the **Vikingemuseet** (Viking Museum).

Northwest of the cathedral, along Vestergåde, stands the Gothic 13th-century **Vor Frue Kirke** (Church of Our Lady), within which are ruins of an earlier stone crypt church (AD 1060). The main church has frescos and a fine altarpiece by Claus Berg (1520). The Gothic cloister leads to the former chapter house, now an old people's home; its walls are covered with medieval secular paintings.

Before you leave the centre,

two modern buildings deserve more than a just a passing glance:

Århus Rådhus (Town Hall) is a marble-clad structure, with an unusual tower designed by Arne Jacobsen and Erik Møller and built in 1941. Guided tours of the council chamber and civic hall show murals from the days of Nazi occupation, painted by Albert Naur, who managed to include some secret symbols. There is a wonderful view of the city and the bay from the 197ft (60m) tower.

Musikhuset (the Concert Hall) was built in 1982 and is the home of the Jutland Opera and Århus Symphony Orchestra. It is a tall glass structure supported inside by slender white pillars, with palm trees to relieve the yellow brickwork. There are free foyer concerts and art exhibitions.

Den Gamle By (the Old Town) is an open-air museum set in a park with its own lake. Over 70 houses and workshops, mostly half-timbered and the oldest of which is 500 years old, have been dismantled from all over Denmark and rebuilt here to recreate a vision of old-style urban life, complete with cobbled streets.

There is a real period atmosphere when the old-fashioned bakers' and grocers' shops are open. It is a relaxing area to visit but can attract large crowds.

While in this part of town, visit the colourful **Botanisk Have** (Botanical Gardens), with its glasshouses and an open-air theatre.

In a large parkland area to the north of Århus lie the university and three more museums, the most interesting of which is **Århus Kunstmuseum** (Art Museum). This museum, in Vennelyst Park, displays Danish paintings from 1750 to the present day and holds regular exhibitions of modern art.

Transport

Several guided bus tours are available: ask at the tourist office. For bus travel, Århus is divided into four zones and offers several types of ticket. The most expensive is a single ticket available from automatic machines at the back of the bus. Better value is a multi-ride ticket, an 11-journey strip card that has to be punched each time you start a journey. Prices vary, depending on the number of zones covered. There is also a family group multi-ride ticket (four rides for up to six passengers) valid outside the rush hour on weekdays and all day at weekends. A 24-hour Tourist Ticket gives unlimited travel, including the sightseeing tour. Tickets are on sale at newsagents, news stands and shops.

Accommodation

There is a good selection of hotels, both in and out of town. Central and inexpensive is the friendly **Hotel Ritz**, near the railway station (tel: 86 13 44 44); much more expensive is the 150-year-old **Royal** (tel: 86 12 00 11), a classical building which has been luxuriously renovated and now operates the casino. The cheapest hotels in town are **Eriksens** (tel: 86 13 62 96) by the station, and the **Park Hotel** in Sønder Alle (tel: 86 12 32 31).

The **Hotel La Tour** (tel: 86 16 78 88) to the north is ideal for families, with comfortable rooms. For a stay on the coast the modern **Hotel Marselis** (tel: 86 14 44 11) on Strandvejen overlooks the sea and has its own swimming pool.

Restaurants

With over 200 places serving food, the choice is wide. **Den Grimme Ælling** (the Ugly Duckling) appropriately serves a lunchtime duckling buffet (not Sundays) including beer or wine, and an evening buffet. The unpretentious **Rådhus Kafeen** is good value. *A la carte* Danish food is served at the attractive **Prins Ferdinand** in the Old Town. You can also eat outside in the courtyard at **Jacob's BarBQ** (Vestergade 3), to the sound of live music in the piano bar. Fish-lovers should head for the **Marselisborg Yacht Harbour** south of Århus and try the **Seafood Restaurant** (tel: 86 18 56 55).

Entertainment

Concerts, operas, plays (in Danish) and ballet alternate on the **Concert Hall**'s two stages. The season at the **Århus Theatre** runs from September to June, and there are other small theatres. There are four cinemas. The monthly publication *Århus This Week*, available from the tourist office, lists events.

There are about a dozen venues for rock and jazz: for

Fine historic buildings are gathered together at Århus Old Town

rock, try **Huset** on Vester Alle or **58** (at Vestergade 58), and for jazz **Glazzhuset Clemensborg**. Several cafés around the cathedral have live music too, with bands or piano bars, while discos and night-clubs are proliferating fast – try **Blitz**, on Klostergade, or the **Road House** at Frederiksgade 76, with dancing and a laser show.

Excursions from Århus

No visit to Århus is complete without paying a courtesy call to the town's oldest and best preserved inhabitant. Found in a peat bot, the Grauballe man, whose Iron Age body dates from 300BC, has dark brown skin lying in loose folds around his thighs, and his small-featured face is fringed with gingery hair.

The body lies in the small **Forhistorisk Museum Moesgård** (Moesgård Prehistoric Museum), about five miles (9km) south of the city. Other exhibits range from the Stone Age to the Vikings, and include some Runic stones. Outside is a countryside trail leading to the sea, passing reconstructed prehistoric dwellings and Stone and Bronze Age burial mounds.

The large wooded area to the south of Århus is the city's playground, for sport and entertainment. Nearest to town is **Tivoli Friheden**, a large amusement park. The southern part of this area, **Marselisborg Skov** (woods) and **Dyrehaven**

(deer park), with sika and fallow deer, is more heavily wooded and crossed by many footpaths.

Marselisborg Slot (Palace), the royal family's summer residence, is near by. Changing of the guard takes place at noon when the family is there. The gardens only are open to the public, when the family is not in residence.

The **Mindeparken** (National Park) and memorial commemorating South Jutland's losses in World War I can also be explored.

There are good beaches at Moesgård and Ballehage (near Marselisberg Skov), both with Blue Flag awards. North of town, you can bathe at Bellevue and den Permanente beaches.

JUTLAND'S ISLANDS

JUTLAND'S ISLANDS

WHAT TO SEE

ANHOLT

This tiny island of 22 square
miles (36 sq km) lies in the
middle of the Kattegat between
Denmark and Sweden, and the
ferry trip from Grenå takes
nearly three hours.
Once occupied by the British
Navy during the Napoleonic
Wars, today Anholt has around
150 inhabitants.
No cars are permitted and
Ørkenen (drifting sands) are the
main feature visible from the
low hills at Nordbjerg. Just north
of here is a sanctuary for
wading birds. The beaches are
good and bikes can be hired.
For accommmodation, there is
one campsite at **Anholt Kro** (tel:
86 31 91 00).

FANØ

A mere 20-minute ferry ride
from Esbjerg, Fanø is 11 miles
(18km) long, and the sandy
beaches of its west coast tend
to draw large crowds. The
islanders bought the island
from the King when he
auctioned it in 1741, and with it
came the right to build sailing
boats. Some of central Fanø is
wooded, and much is covered
with holiday homes and
campsites.

Sightseeing

In Nordby, the **Fanø Søfarts-og
Dragtudstilling Museum**
(Seafaring and National
Costume Museum) displays
model ships and local dress,
and the **Fanø Museum** displays

the islanders' lifestyle 300 years
ago and shows sailors'
souvenirs. Model ships are
suspended from the ceiling of
the 18th-century church. The
prettiest village is Sønderho,
with its windmill, old thatched
houses and narrow streets.

Accommodation and
Restaurants

There are nine campsites and
four holiday centres on Fanø.
Sønderho Kro (tel: 75 16 40 09)
is full of character and serves
good food.
Fanø Krogård at Nordby is a
cosy 17th-century inn (tel: 75 16
20 52) serving good meals, and
you can also eat at **Kellers
Hotel** by the sea.
In Sønderho, **Kromanns
Fiskeresturant** (tel: 75 16 44
45) specialises in fish dishes,
and at Nordby, **Restaurant
Fanø Krogård** is a cosy 17th-
century inn (tel: 75 16 20 52).

LÆSØ

An hour-and-a-half ferry trip
from Frederikshavn on Jutland
brings you to Læsø, 44 sq miles
(114 sq km) and exactly the
same size as Samsø, but with
only half its population – some
2,550 souls. The ferry lands at
Vesterø Havn, where it is met
by a bus which will take you the
five miles (8km) to Byrum.
The island is ideal for nature-
lovers: three quarters of it is
wild, with woods, moorland and
sand dunes. Wild flowers are
abundant and include orchids.
In the south are salt marshes,
and wading birds live in a
group of islets off that coast.
Daily visits can be made here
by tractor-bus which starts from

Byrum. The Knotten peninsula
in the northeast is also a bird
sanctuary. The best sandy
beaches are on the long north
coast and many have been
awarded Blue Flags.

Sightseeing

Læsø's most unusual feature is
the seaweed-thatched roofs on
many farmhouses in the chief
town of Byrum. Even the half-
timbered **Museumsgården**
(local museum), nearly 400
years old, has a seaweed
thatch. The tower by the
Romanesque church has a view
over the whole island.

The **Fiskeri og Søfartsmuseet**
(Fishing and Maritime Museum)
at Byrum displays seafaring
items.

Accommodation and
Restaurants

Hotels to aim for include
Lærkely (tel: 98 49 81 66) in
Byrum and **Havnebakken** (tel:
98 49 90 09) in Vesterø Havn.

Safe harbour for yachts on Samsø

SAMSØ

Situated in the Kattegat, halfway
between Jutland, Zealand and
Funen, Samsø is a delightfully
rural, bottle-shaped island,
particularly rich in birdlife.
White churches and small
villages with thatched cottages
are scattered over the island.
The inland scenery ranges from
moors to forest, while the coast
offers cliffs and sandy beaches.
There is much rich farmland
which is intensively cultivated.
The potatoes are reputed to be
the best in Denmark and in late
summer the trusting locals put
flowers, fruit and vegetables
outside their houses for sale.
Samsø is a popular holiday
resort and many homes are
rented out for the summer,
even the thatched ones. The
island is easily accessible from
Hov on Jutland (to Sælvig – 1
hour 20 minutes on the ferry) or
from Kalundborg on Zealand (to
Kolby Kås – 2 hours). You can
hire a bicycle at Sælvig and at

Kolby Kås to explore the island, or you can catch the bus, which meets the ferry and stops at many places.

Sightseeing

The chief town is Tranebjerg, which has little of note apart from a 14th-century church, and a large defence tower with holes from which tar and hot water were poured on invaders in the Middle Ages. The **museum** illustrates local rural life.

Nordby is a captivating village where the half-timbered thatched cottages, with their tiny windows, stand higgledy-piggledy, except those which overlook the large village pond. The church is half a mile (1km) away – the villages it served are long since abandoned – so Nordby has a separate bell tower. Tracks lead to the beach, or you can go further north to **Nordby Bakker**, a nature reserve, with marked walks. **Ballebjerg** is the highest point on Samsø, with good views from its lookout tower. **Besser Rev**, on the east, is a reef encircling the lagoon of Stavns Fjord, now a bird reserve. Other sights include a restored post mill at Brundby, and the 15th-century church at Onsbjerg with a gold crucifix dating from 1200.

Accommodation and Restaurants

Flinch's Hotel at Tranebjerg (tel: 86 59 17 22) has recently been renovated and serves good food. **Nordby Kro**, in Nordby (tel: 86 59 60 86), is a cottage-style building with a restaurant.

BORNHOLM

Bornholm has belonged to Denmark since 1658, when much of southern Sweden was under Danish rule. The island lies 95 miles (153km) southeast of Copenhagen – a seven-hour ferry trip to Rønne, the main town. Bornholm is rhomboid in shape and larger than many other islands, but still only 25 miles (40km) between its most distant corners. It consists of granite which gives rise to rugged coastal cliffs; in the hilly interior are heathland and woods, ponds and marshes as well as cultivated fields. Prehistoric remains include burial mounds and rune stones. Round churches from the 12th and 13th centuries, whitewashed and fortified, are a feature.

Bornhom is an attractive island, well worth visiting. Fine sandy beaches, ancient villages, museums, together with varied walking and three golf courses, make it a popular summer resort. The mild climate produces unusual fauna and flora, and the island is a noted stopover for migrating birds.

WHAT TO SEE

Rønne, the main town, is full of tiny dark red or ochre-coloured half-timbered houses lining

Bornholm has always been an important trading centre and today's islanders earn their living from fishing and fish processing – the **Bornholmer**, a smoked herring, is highly recommended.

The round Nykirke, on Bornholm

narrow cobbled streets round the lively harbour. The **Bornholm Museum** displays a collection of local prehistoric and geological finds, as well as an old grocer's shop, toys, costumes, clocks and ceramics. The art museum in the same building has paintings from 1800. **Erichsens Gård** is an early 19th-century furnished merchant's house.

The oldest of the four circular churches is at **Nyker**, with frescos round the top of the central pillar and a rune stone in the porch. **Hasle**, site of the annual herring festival, is another quaint village, with a **Smokehouse Museum**. **Sandvig** and **Allinge** are two medieval fishing villages with narrow, twisting streets and busy harbours. Sandvig also has a wide, sandy beach. At **Madsebakke** is a group of old rock carvings. Thirteenth-century **Hammershus Castle**, once Scandinavia's largest fortress, is now an impressive,

overgrown ruin of red brick towers and turrets on cliffs overlooking the sea.

The road descends steeply to Gudhjem (ferries go from here to the island of **Christiansø**, a former naval base) which still has some smokehouses. Just beyond, at Melsted, is **Melstedgård**, where 18th- and 19th-century half-timbered farm buildings form a living agricultural museum, with demonstrations of traditional farming methods. At **Østerlars** you will find the largest of the round churches, and the best-preserved is at Nylars. **Svaneke** is a prosperous market town with an attractive harbour. At **Dueodde** is the island's best and largest beach, part of a large dune area backed by pinewoods. The sand is so fine it is used in egg-timers; once it was sold as 'writers' sand', to dry ink. Numerous campsites and holiday homes indicate the area's popularity.

Inland at **Åkirkeby**, the island's oldest market town, is a 12th-century stone church with impressive Romanesque carving on the sandstone font.

Accommodation and Restaurants

The **Hotel Griffen** in Rønne (tel: 56 95 51 11) is comfortable and central. At Svaneke, try the small **Hotel Munke** (tel: 56 49 61 12); both have restaurants. In Dueodde, **Hotel Bornholm** (tel: 56 48 83 83) has a fine outlook. Accommodation is also available in private houses, but you may have to stay for a minimum of three days.

ZEALAND (SJÆLLAND)

This is Denmark's biggest and most densely populated island and where much of the country's industry is concentrated, particularly in the north. The area has some spectacular castles, and the coast is sandy, but public beaches near the capital tend to get crowded. The southern part of Zealand is more rural and includes some historic towns.

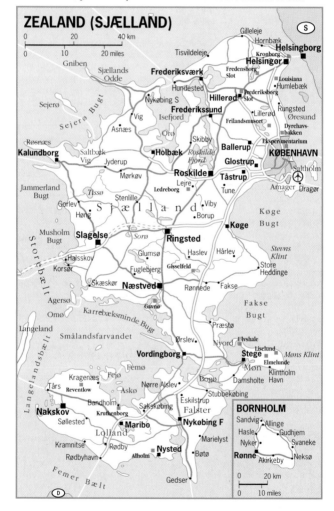

ZEALAND (SJÆLLAND)

WHAT TO SEE

◆◆◆
FREDERIKSBORG SLOT ✓
(CASTLE)

At Hillerød, is the fairy-tale castle built (1600–20) on three islands by Christian IV, with an excess of spires, gables and copper-green roofs. He demolished the previous castle on the site, which had been built in 1560 by his father, Frederik II as a hunting base. A large part of Christian's castle was burnt down during the last century and the present castle is a faithful reconstruction of his masterpiece.

In 1878 it became **Det Nationalhistoriske Museum** (National Historical Museum), covering 500 years of Danish history.

The castle's years of glory were between 1671 and 1840, when it was the home of all Danish monarchs and they were crowned in the chapel. Its 60 rooms contain a superb collection of paintings, furniture and tapestries by the best European painters and craftspeople of their day. The most magnificent rooms include the huge Riddersalen (Knights' Hall), with a richly decorated vaulted ceiling supported by marble columns, and the splendid Great Hall or Audience Chamber, every inch decorated with gold.

The original chapel wing was designed for royal use, so the most valuable materials were used: the nave vaults are gilded and the king's closed pew is inlaid with rare woods.

The black marble gallery served as the knights' chapel, and is hung with rows of shields. The ebony ceiling in the royal oratories is decorated with ivory rosettes. Even the smaller rooms are richly and tastefully decorated and filled with antiques.

The gardens which surround the castle and the lake are worth seeing.

The ornate ceiling of the Great Hall is echoed in floor and wall decor

Helsingør is still a major ferry port

◆◆◆
HELSINGØR

Helsingør's early prosperity was based on its position at the neck of the Øresund, which separates Denmark from Sweden. From 1427 until 1857 all ships passing through had to pay dues to the ruler of the Sound. Many rich merchants settled here, and the grid-patterned streets lined with charming half-timbered houses still stand.

Sightseeing

Helsingør is Elsinore, home of Shakespeare's Hamlet, who was probably named after the Danish mythological figure, Amleth. **Kronborg Castle**, in a dramatic coastal setting overlooking Øresund, was originally built in the 15th century and still retains its huge bastions and medieval ramparts. It was rebuilt several times and was finally restored to its 17th-century grandeur in the 1920s.

The royal apartments are sparsely furnished with early,

heavy Dutch and Danish pieces, and there is no comfort in the bare floors and stone staircases, but the ceilings are painted and valuable oil paintings and Flemish tapestries cover the walls. The empty, oak-beamed Great Hall is one of the largest in Europe: its walls are hung with scenes of Kronborg by the 17th-century painter Isaac Isaacsz.

The chapel survived the fire of 1629 – its rich carvings and gilded wood contrast with the white vaulted ceiling.

Guided tours of the casemates reveal them to be dark, dank and cobbled. Here sits the statue of **Holger Danske**, Denmark's national hero, a Viking contemporary of the Emperor Charlemagne, said to have fought in the French wars, who, legend has it, will rise again in Denmark's hour of need. At one time the casemates housed a brewery, and the horse and wagon area are still visible.

Even deeper below ground is a former prison, full of bats, and a huge room vast enough to store six weeks' provisions for 1,000 soldiers.

Walk round the bastions before you go – soldiers guard the cannons from their sentry boxes – and remember where the ghost of Hamlet's father trod.

Handels-og Søfartsmuseet (Commercial and Maritime Museum) is also at Kronborg (castle ticket admits you). Its large collection on several floors covers Danish shipping and trade from 1400 to the present day, with full-size and model ships, figureheads, a stoker's room and old navigation equipment.

In the 15th century three monasteries were founded at Helsingør, and the large red brick Carmelite building of **Sct Mariæ**, where the composer Dietrich Buxtehude was organist, is said to be the best preserved medieval monastery in northern Europe.

The small hospital for seamen, built by the Carmelites, is now **Helsingør Bymuseum** (Town Museum) which displays local items. The larger, but equally old **Sct Olai Kirke** (St Olav's Church), now a cathedral, features a magnificent altarpiece.

Accommodation and Restaurants

Hotel Hamlet (with Restaurant Ophelia!) is comfortable and near the castle (tel: 49 21 05 91). **Klostercafeen** is good for lunch, and for dinner **Anno 1880** is a half-timbered house near Kronborg (tel: 49 21 54 80). There are several eating places along Stengåde.

Crossing to Sweden

The boat trip to Sweden (Helsingborg) from Helsingør lasts only 25 minutes (there are two or three departures every hour). Don't be surprised to see lots of Swedes in Helsingør – they are there to take advantage of Denmark's cheaper daily commodities, including meat, cheese and alcohol.

Excursions from Helsingør

Completed in 1776, **Fredensborg** (Castle of Peace) is a fine example of Danish architecture, built by Frederik IV to celebrate the end of the war with Sweden in 1720. Appropriately, it is in grand country house style rather than fortified, and is now used by the royal family in spring and autumn. A few rooms are open to the public in July, but its extensive park and gardens, on the edge of Esrum Sø, Denmark's second biggest lake, are open all year.

Marienlyst Slot (Castle), stands north of Helsingør station. First built as a retreat (Lundehave) for Frederik II, it was redesigned in 1760 for the widow of Frederik V by the French architect N H Jardin. Original Louis XVI interiors with period furniture fill the top floor, and there are lovely collections of paintings and silver. Hamlet's grave is in the garden.

◆
KALUNDBORG

Kalundborg is perhaps better known for its radio transmitter or as a ferry port to Århus than for its well-preserved medieval centre and outstanding 12th-century church. **Vor Frue Kirke** (Church of Our Lady) is shaped like a Greek cross, with five brick towers, each topped by a green copper spire. Other medieval buildings near the church include **Den Gamle Tiendelade** (Old Tithe Barn), the Gothic **Borgerhus** (Citizen's House) and some prettily restored small houses.

Kalundborg og Omegns

Museum (Museum of Kalundborg and the Environs) is housed in the former mansion of Lindegaarden, built around 1500, and holds a good collection of national costumes, craftsmen's tools and farmhouse interiors.

Accommodation and Restaurants

Ole Lunds Gård (tel: 53 51 01 65) is central, with a restaurant; near the station is **Restaurant Fjorden** with Café Vigen. **Bromølle Kro** (tel: 53 55 00 90) is an old thatched inn at Jyderup, south of the town.

KØGE

Køge is a charming town with a cobbled market square, many timber-framed houses and medieval cellars.

Originally founded in the 13th century as a port, exporting grain to the Baltic towns, Køge prospered in the Middle Ages. But in the early 17th century, fires and the war against Sweden ravaged both its buildings and its population. The old harbour is now used by yachts as well as for trade and ship repairs.

Sightseeing

The roads leading from Torvet (the market square) are lined with half-timbered houses built after the last fire in 1663; the oldest dated house in Denmark (1527) is at **Kirkestræde 20**. **St Nikolai Kirke** (St Nicholas Church) is constructed in Gothic-style brickwork, and has a medieval fresco and many painted epitaphs.

Køge Museum, situated in 17th-century half-timbered buildings round a courtyard, displays locally excavated items such as coins, as well as embroidery and utensils, and two typically furnished living rooms from 1800 and 1900.

Accommodation

Hotel Niels Juel is a new hotel, built in warehouse style, overlooking the harbour (tel: 56 63 18 00), and **Søvilla Kro and Motel** (tel: 53 66 15 14) lies north of the town.

Restaurants

Two historic restaurants worth visiting are **Christians Minde** (tel: 56 63 12 31) in an old merchant's yard, and **Richters** (tel: 53 66 29 49), in a timber framed building.

LOUISIANA MUSEUM

Louisiana Museum for Moderne Kunst (Museum of Modern Art) at Humlebæk is a clever combination of art, sculpture and landscape, based on the collection of art-lover Knud Jensen.

The museum is housed in a beautiful hilltop villa and park, with metal sculptures dotted around lawns sloping down to the sea. The pictures, dating from the 1950s, are by artists within the COBRA (see **Silkeborg**, Jutland) and Constructivism movements. A new underground Graphic Art wing joins the two existing buildings. American artists, such as Roy Lichtenstein and Andy Warhol are well represented.

It's thumbs up for modern art

♦♦♦
ROSKILDE ✓

Roskilde's history goes back to
the Vikings. From the 12th
century, when Bishop Absalon
founded the cathedral, the town
enjoyed great power and
prosperity as the centre of the
Danish Catholic church and
residence of the Danish royal
court.

It was also the capital of
Denmark until 1400, and
although the court moved to
Copenhagen, all Danish
monarchs have been buried
here since the 15th century.
After the Reformation (1536) the
town declined, and did not
revive until the arrival of the
railway in 1847.

Today Roskilde is an important
commercial centre and
university town.

Sightseeing
Domkirken (the Cathedral)
was built on the site of Harald
Bluetooth's first wooden church
(about 960). Bishop Absalon's
cathedral was established in
1170, a red brick building in
Romanesque and Gothic styles.

Its towers and green copper
spires were added at a later
date. The cathedral's interior is
light and fairly plain, but
enriched by the fine gilded
altar screen and a pulpit of
marble and alabaster.

More impressive than the
architecture are the 38 **royal
tombs**, from Queen Margrete
(who died in 1412) to the father
of the present queen, Frederik
IX (who died in 1972), and
whose grave is marked by a
granite slab outside the
cathedral. The other royal
remains are inside chapels, in
sarcophagi which display
various degrees of richness –
marble, silver and bronze.
Particularly interesting are the
large neoclassical chapel of
Frederik V, the decorated and
vaulted chapel of Christian IV,
and that of Christian I, where a
granite pillar is marked with the
height of various kings,
including Peter the Great.

The former **Palæsamlingerne**
(Bishop's Palace), linked to the
cathedral by an archway, has a
collection of furniture and

paintings from 18th- and 19th-century merchants' homes.

Brødrene Lützhøfts Købmandsgård (Lützhoft's Brothers' General Store) is a small and unusual museum of the 1920s, cluttered with goods as varied as rope, herrings, clogs and sugarloaves, all for sale.

One of the greatest finds of recent years is housed in **Vikingeskibshallen** (the Viking Ship Museum), Strandengen, at the edge of the fjord.

The museum itself is a disconcertingly modern structure, one side of glass almost bringing the fjord into the building, and displays the black remains of five Viking sailing ships which were sunk across the narrow neck in about AD1000 to prevent the enemy's fleets of ships from attacking the town.

The ships were discovered in 1957 and raised in 1962; since then the vessels have undergone a lengthy process of conservation and reconstruction, with the missing parts now indicated in metal. *MS Sagafjord* runs boat trips on Roskilde Fjord.

Accommodation

Hotel Prindsen, in the centre of town at Algåde 13, is an elegant and comfortable hotel (tel: 42 35 80 10) with a good restaurant. **Svogerslev Kro** (tel: 46 38 30 05) is further out of town to the west, a lovely old thatched building in pleasant surroundings.

Osted Kro (tel: 42 39 70 41), to the southwest in Osted, has been extended.

Restaurants

Club 42, Skomagergade 42 (tel:42 35 17 64) serves Danish food.

There is a bird's-eye view over the fjord from **Restaurant Toppen** (tel:42 36 04 12). A good value Sunday lunch buffet is available at **Scandic Hotel** restaurant (tel:46 32 46 32).

Excursions from Roskilde

Ledreborg Slot og Park (Ledreborg Castle and Park) is an 18th-century Versailles-style palace set in a terraced park at the end of a long tree-lined avenue, six miles (10km) west of Roskilde.

It has been the home of the Holstein–Ledreborg family since 1739, and the fine rooms contain excellent paintings, chandeliers, tapestries and gilded furniture; there is a beautiful baroque chapel and an old kitchen and there are spectacular views over the river valley.

The **Historisk-Arkæologisk Forsøgcenter** (Historical Archeological Experimental Centre) at Lejre is a ponderous title for a delightful place. Set in wooded hills about six miles (10 km) west of Roskilde, a Stone Age field, an Iron Age village and 19th-century farm cottages have recently been constructed to provide an understanding of early

---

Good-value Tourist Tickets
The Copenhagen Card covers the main sights in Roskilde and Ledregorg Castle, and includes free travel from Copenhagen.

agricultural methods, crafts and building.

In summer it is occupied and worked by volunteers, who carry out such tasks as logging, corn-grinding, blacksmithing and pottery.

Ancient breeds of domestic animals are kept and worked as they would have been in the past.

◆◆◆
RUNGSTED

Fans of *Out of Africa*, the creation of novelist Karen Blixen (alias Isak Dinesen), should not fail to visit Rungstedlund, the childhood home to which she returned from Africa in 1931, after the collapse of her farming venture, and where she remained until her death in 1962.

The large, gracious house, on the coast between Copenhagen and Helsingøre, is now the **Karen Blixen Museum**.

The former stables house an evocative display of photographs of the author, from her Danish childhood to a wrinkled old age, often in the company of the famous, and including her life in Africa.

She wrote in English, rewriting her work in Danish for publication, and many of her manuscripts and letters home are on display, as well as a library of her works.

Guided tours (overshoes compulsory) include the rooms where Karen Blixen lived and wrote, unchanged since her death: the cosy green study, overlooking the garden, the comfortable drawing room, the writing room, with its fine view

of the harbour and its Masai spears and other souvenirs of Africa.

Karen Blixen was also a talented artist, and a small collection of her paintings, done in Africa and Denmark, may be seen.

She preserved the 40-acre (16-ha) park as a bird sanctuary, and she was laid to rest beneath a simple stone slab under a beech tree in the northwest corner

◆◆◆
VORDINGBORG

Vordingborg, in the southwest of Zealand, is linked to the island of Falster by a bridge. Most of the town is modern, but the **Gasetårnet** (Goose Tower), which stands on a grassy hill, is the only survivor of four corner towers of the curtain wall which surrounded a 12th-century castle (later demolished). Valdemar Atterdag decreed that a gilded goose should crown the tower, as an insult to the towns of the Hanseatic League. Climb the Goose Tower for fine views, and walk along by the walls.

A herb garden and the former cavalry barracks, now the **South Zealand Museum** are close by. **Bellavista** is a modern art gallery, situated in a former mansion.

Accommodation and Restaurants

Hotel Kong Valdemar at Algåde 101 (tel: 53 77 00 95) is near the Goose Tower and **Udby Kro** (tel: 53 78 10 02), one of Denmark's oldest inns, about six miles (10km) north, offers a good choice of food.

NORTH ZEALAND COAST

The sandy beaches of the north coast provide an easy summer escape from Copenhagen and many Danes own summer-houses here. Without a car, you can get to the resorts below by train, then it's about 15 minutes walk to the sea.

WHAT TO SEE

◆
GILLELEJE
Gilleleje is Denmark's northernmost point, a popular resort and the largest fishing port in Zealand. Fish auctions are held here on weekdays. A footpath runs along the top of the dunes to **Gilbjerg Hoved** from where there is a spectacular view. A memorial stands here, to the philosopher Søren Kierkegaard.
Nakkehoved Øster Fyr (the Lighthouse) was built in 1772, and is the only preserved coal-fired lighthouse in the world. Inland, Gilleleje has many old half-timbered, thatched houses, two museums devoted to the local fishing industry, and a simple 16th-century church.

Accommodation and Restaurants
The pleasant **Hotel Strand** is Gilleleje's only hotel and overlooks the sea (tel: 48 30 05 12). **Gilleleje Havn** is a fish restaurant by the harbour and **Fyrkroen**, near the lighthouse at Nakkehoved, serves cold table lunches at weekends.

◆◆
HORNBÆK
Hornbaek is another former fishing village which is now a popular summer resort, its beaches and dunes backed by thick woods, planted nearly 200 years ago to provide protection from frequent gales. In the little town, passages wind between the old red and yellow fishermen's houses, leading up to the 18th-century sailors' church with its collection of model ships.

Accommodation and Restaurants
Hotel Trouville (tel: 42 20 22 00) is close to the forest and beach and has an indoor pool. **Søstrene Olsen** (tel: 42 20 05 50) is a seafood restaurant close to the harbour.

NÆSTVED
Try to visit Næstved on a Wednesday morning when the colourful cavalry squadron of the Royal Hussars (who accompany the royal family on state occasions) ride through the town blowing trumpets. Næstved is the largest town in South Zealand and is steeped in history. Situated at a fjord and river junction it has easy access to the sea and until the 17th century traded with Norway, Scotland and Germany. The port was later expanded to take bigger ships.

Sightseeing
The town grew up round a Benedictine monastery, founded in 1135, in an attractive riverside setting. Since the Reformation this building has served as a boarding school called **Herlufsholm,** after its founder, Herluf Trolle. The

adjoining red brick church was restored and enlarged in the 13th century. Inside is an ivory crucifix from the same date, an ornate altar, and the splendid sarcophagus of the founder. Medieval Næstved is about two miles (2.5km) south of the monastery, with cobbled streets and low, half-timbered houses huddled round the restored Gothic **Sct Peders Kirke** (St Peter's Church), the largest in Denmark. It has vaulted ceilings, a fresco of King Valdemar Atterdag (1340–75) and medieval choir stalls. Yet a third medieval church still stands – **Sct Mortens** (St Martins), with a large and wonderfully carved altarpiece. This church adjoins one of the many half-timbered houses,

Apostelhuset, and a row of medieval brick houses (Boderne) with arched windows and is now part of **Næstved Museum**, displaying some of the glass and ceramics for which the town is renowned. Another part of the museum, in the Helligåndshuset (House of the Holy Spirit) exhibits church sculptures.

You can visit the old Kähler ceramic works in the town, and the world-famous **Holmegaards Glasværker** (Glassworks) and museum.

Accommodation and Restaurants

Hotel Vinhuset, 200 years old with a vaulted cellar, but modernised and comfortable, is central (tel: 53 72 08 07).
Menstrup Kro is just as old, but about eight miles (12km) west

The unusual church at Kalundborg

of Næstved, with an indoor pool and a good restaurant (tel: 53 74 30 03). **Restaurant Fiskerhuset** (tel: 53 64 60 11) specialises in fish, while **Herlufholmskovens** (tel: 53 72 74 43), in the woods north of town, provides traditional Danish food. In Næstved, **Det Røde Pakhus** on Riddergåde and **Rådhuskroen** on Skomagerrækken, are both reliable.

Excursions from Næstved

On a small island about five miles (8km) southwest of Næstved lies **Gavnø**, an 18th-century house and garden built on the site of a former convent. The rococo-style house has an outstanding collection of pictures by Danish and foreign artists, fine 18th- and 19th-century examples of European furniture, and the small and colourful former convent chapel. In the extensive and well maintained grounds is a rose garden. There are also collections of fire engines and tropical butterflies.

About 10 miles (16km) north-east of Næstved is **Gisselfeld**, a 16th-century red brick Renaissance castle in a breathtaking lakeside setting. The swans here inspired Hans Christian Andersen to write his fairy tale *The Ugly Duckling*. The castle is not open, but the large English-style wooded park is.

◆

TISVILDELEJE

Tisvildeleje is an attractive and often crowded resort, with beaches of white sand. South of the village is **Tisvilde Hegn**, a forest of gnarled trees planted in the last century to stabilise the drifting sand. There are good walks along the coast and views across to Sweden.

Accommodation

Højbohus (tel: 42 30 71 19) is a comfortable hotel.

Viking ships preserved at Roskilde

ZEALAND'S ISLANDS

The three large, green and rather flat islands off the south coast of Zealand – Falster, Lolland and Møn – are within easy reach of Copenhagen, and can also be reached from Germany and Funen.

WHAT TO SEE

FALSTER

Falster has a few good beaches on the east coast, many flying the Blue Flag; one of the most popular is Marielyst.

The main town, Nykøbing F, is a lively place with pavement cafés, street theatre and a mini-zoo in **Folkeparken** (free). Of several medieval buildings, the most notable is the half-timbered Czarens Hus (Tsar's House), named after Peter the Great's visit. It now houses **Museet Falsters Minder** (the Falster Memorial Museum) and displays local historical and archaeological finds. Energetic visitors can climb the water tower in Hollands Gård.

LOLLAND

Lolland is Denmark's third largest island, flat apart from some gentle hills in the north-west, and fertile, producing large quantities of sugar beet. The island is scattered with large estates, some of which are open to the public, and there are some excellent beaches around Kramnitse.

Sightseeing

The largest town is Nakskov, home of Denmark's biggest sugar refinery. Between the market square, with its 17th-century pharmacy, and the harbour, is a picturesque area of narrow lanes with half-timbered houses and old shops. The tall spire of **Sct Nikolai Kirke** (St Nicholas Church) dominates the town – a Swedish canonball, fired in 1659, is lodged in the chancel arch. Near Pederstrup is **Reventlow-Museet**, set in an English-style park. This classical building was the family home of C D F Reventlow (1748–1827), famous for his role in liberating the peasants and education reform. Maribo is a delightful town with cobbled sreets, pastel-coloured cottages and a red brick cathedral by a lake. **Maribo Domkirke** (Cathedral) was formerly the abbey church, founded in 1416 and restored in the last century. Its white rib-vaulted interior sets off the painted Renaissance pulpit and ornate gold altar. All that remains of the convent built at the same time are pillar bases, once part of the nuns' cloister and refectory, standing between cathedral and lake. For a totally un-Danish experience, visit **Knuthenborg Safari Park**, where 800 species of animals and birds, including giraffes, emus, and rhinos, graze amongst the chewed-off tree trunks. **Småland** (Miniworld) is a children's amusement park.

Accommodation

In Maribo the new **Hotel Dana** (tel: 53 88 17 11) and **Ebsens Hotel** (tel: 53 88 10 44) are both very central and comfortable, while the large **Hotel Hvide Hus** (tel: 53 88 10 11) overlooks the lakes. **Hotel Harmonien** at Nakskov (tel: 53 92 21 00) is central and suitable for families. **Hotel og Restaurant** at Skovridergaarden (tel: 53 92 03 55) is an old country inn.

Restaurants

In Maribo, **Bangs Have** (tel: 53 88 19 11) overlooks the harbour, while **Skaanings Gaard** is central and offers *à la carte* dishes. **Restaurant Lysemose** (tel: 53 88 02 14) is an old thatched building. In Nakskov, try **Vinkæ Ideren** for a choice of fish dishes

Excursions from Lolland

Near Nysted, 12th-century **Aalholm Slot** (Castle) is one of the oldest inhabited castles in the country and has finely furnished rooms, a torture chamber and a family ghost. In the grounds is the **Automobil-museum** (Car Museum), one of Denmark's largest collections of veteran cars. A steam train runs from here to the beach.

Another steam train, **Museumsbanen**, chugs across Lolland from Bandholm to Maribo on summer weekends. You can explore the **Maribo Lakes** by boat or walk round them on marked trails. Boats sail from Kragenæs to nearby islands (Fejø and Femø) and from Bandholm to the island of Askø, while the post boat sails to little islands in Nakskov Fjord.

◆◆◆
MØN

This is the prettiest of the three islands, the most rural and least accessible. The steep chalk cliffs on the east coast (**Møns Klint**) are particularly dramatic: fossils can be found at the base and rare orchids in the woods above. **Klintholm Havn**, a small fishing village, and **Liselund Manor**, built in the 18th century, are both worth visiting. Liselund is thatched and beautifully furnished. In the pleasant park are three unusual summer houses – Hans Christian Andersen is said to have written *The Tinderbox* in one of them. Neolithic people inhabited Møn, and long barrows (including **Kong Askers Høj**) and Bronze Age tombs are scattered around the island.

So are medieval whitewashed churches, particularly interesting for their frescos of country life. Fanefjord, Keldby, Stege and the recently restored Elmelunde churches are the best.

Stege is the main town, with preserved medieval ramparts, and the **Møn Museum** is a repository of local finds.

The Ulvshale peninsula was Denmark's first nature reserve and is still a bird breeding ground. From here, visit the tiny island of Nyord where farms and field systems have barely changed in 300 years.

Accommodation and Restaurants

A large holiday complex at Klintholm harbour, **Danland på Møn**, offers self-catering accommodation (tel: 55 81 90 55), or you can stay in style at **Liselund Ny Slot** (tel: 55 81 20 81), near the manor house, with a good restaurant. There are also bed and breakfast places.

Peace and Quiet

*Wildlife and
Countryside in Denmark
by Paul Sterry*

As a general rule, the more geographical variety a country has, the more diverse its plant and animal life, and hence the greater its natural history interest. With this in mind, Denmark might seem a rather unpromising destination since it is uniformly low-lying (most of the land being less than 400 feet (120m) above sea level) and has little natural habitat left. But, in fact, Denmark has a lot to offer the visitor interested in natural history, especially one whose interests also embrace geology and archaeology.

In geographical terms, Denmark is fragmented: in addition to its main land mass (the Jutland peninsula), there are more than 400 islands. This means that the coastline is extensive.

The entire landscape, given its basic 'shape' by the effects of glaciation, has been heavily modified by humans. Across the country, there are archaeological remains that remind visitors of the long settlement of Denmark, and examples of modern farming practices are reminders of contemporary land use – nearly three-quarters of the land is agricultural. However, there are still some remnant areas of natural habitats – dunes, freshwater marshes, heaths and forests – and, fortunately, much of Denmark's wildlife is adaptable, many birds, for example, living in comparative harmony with the altered landscape.

*A red-backed shrike, one of many
woodland species to be seen here*

PEACE AND QUIET

Not surprisingly, visiting birdwatchers will find most interest in the coastal birds. Waders, gulls, terns, ducks and geese are abundant, although the species to be seen vary throughout the year. Some are summer visitors while others are year-round residents. Spring and autumn are particularly rewarding because hundreds of thousands of other species pass through on migration. Interesting plant life is more or less confined to coastal districts and small areas of natural or semi-natural habitat protected by reserve status.

In and Around Copenhagen

Although Copenhagen is a bustling modern city, it has several havens of tranquility with a natural history interest. Birdwatchers will find that small, wooded parks have many interesting species – mainly in spring and summer – and parkland lakes, canals and waterfronts have birds throughout the year. Woodland birds may include barred warblers and thrush nightingales. The latter are rather secretive, but visitors cannot fail to miss their loud song, often sung after dark. Lakes and waterways have grebes, ducks, geese and terns in the summer months. In winter, many birds leave and fly south, to be replaced by other, more hardy species. Look for several species of gulls as well as lots of ducks. One of the more regularly encountered is the smew. This small diving duck has mostly white plumage in the male, and grey plumage with a chestnut head in the female. They are often found on surprisingly small areas of water.

Although almost any suitable looking area of woodland or lake is worth exploring, some of the better birdwatching spots in and around Copenhagen are as follows:

Fredriksberg Have – woodland and formal gardens
Utterslev Mose – woods and freshwater in a parkland setting
Amager – an island to the south of Copenhagen.
Look for coastal birds in the fishing village of Dragør and woodland birds in Kongelunden.

Woodland Birds

Spring is the best time of year to look for woodland birds in Denmark. Many of the breeding species are summer migrants, flying south to their wintering grounds in August and September.
Several species of warblers can be seen, the smallest being the willow warbler, whose song is a delightful, descending trill, and the chiffchaff, whose song is exactly like its name. Icterine warblers and barred warblers are also widespread, the latter often being found in close proximity to red-backed shrikes in areas of scrub vegetation. Nuthatches and several species of tits are year-round residents, as is Denmark's most distinctive bird, the crow-sized black woodpecker.

PEACE AND QUIET

Environmental Credentials

Like its neighbouring Scandinavian states, Denmark has a reputation for cleanliness, and is justifiably proud of its 'green' record. But, like all western countries, it has environmental problems and controversies.

For example, the North Sea, a vital component of the economies of all northern European countries, is over-fished and polluted. Only concerted action can reverse the steady deterioration of what used to be one of the world's richest fishing grounds. Intensive farming is revealing its true colours, here as elsewhere. For example, Denmark produces huge quantities of pig meat, but the pigs themselves produce equally spectacular amounts of liquid and solid waste. In a country as small as Denmark, its disposal is an increasingly serious issue. Again, only determined action can solve these growing problems.

The Rebild Hills, a national park

Skagen Nature Reserve

This reserve lies at the far north of the Jutland peninsula and embraces an extensive area of dune formations. To reach it, drive north on route 45. From Frederikshavn, take the coastal road north via Ålbæk to Skagen and Grenen. Access to the reserve is unrestricted and there are plenty of opportunities for extensive walking.

Although the reserve has wildlife interest throughout the year, it is best known as a location for observing migrating birds. Spring is considered to be the best season – April and May in particular – when birds such as thrushes, finches and crows arrive in large numbers from the south and fly north to Norway and Sweden. Birds of prey often pass through in large numbers and waders, gulls and terns can be seen around the shores.

PEACE AND QUIET

Bird Migration
Every spring and autumn, Denmark witnesses bird migration on a grand scale. Many species – especially insect-eaters – are only summer visitors to northern Europe, flying south in the autumn to escape the harsh winters and poor food supplies. Denmark not only receives birds that breed on its own land but also thousands more that are on their way to Norway and Sweden. In spring, many of the migrants funnel up the Jutland peninsula and become concentrated in the Skagen area (at the northern tip). In autumn, the peninsula tip is often the first landfall for tired migrants heading south.

Ringkøbing Fjord
The west coast of Jutland is famous for its fjord landscape and makes an attractive tour for any visitor. Almost anywhere in the region can be good for coastal wildlife, but this, the largest fjord, is generally regarded as the best. It is also the site of an important nature reserve (Tipperne), where an excellent variety of wildfowl and waders can be seen. Ringkøbing Fjord lies roughly 100 miles (60km) north of Esbjerg. A minor road runs more or less around the whole of its margins. From the town of Ringkøbing, drive south to Skjern and Ådum, 31 miles (50km) and then west towards Nørre Bork. At Nymindegab a road runs north to the Tipperne Nature Reserve. If you continue on the main road to the coast, the route heads north along Holmsland Klit to Nørre Lyngvig, and this stretch of the route affords excellent views through the dunes across the fjord and over the North Sea. There is a museum with natural history exhibits near the lighthouse at Nørre Lyngvig. At one time, Ringkøbing Fjord would have been contiguous with the North Sea, but a sand

Sand dunes at Agger Tange

bar has built up which now separates the two bodies of water. Although a small inlet breaches the sand bar, allowing salt water in, the waters of the fjord are essentially fresh.

Tipperne Nature Reserve

This is on a small peninsula in the southernmost part of Ringkøbing Fjord. Here you will find an information centre, observation tower and a series of marked footpaths. During the summer months typical wetland birds breed here, including black-tailed godwits, ruffs, curlews, avocets, terns and Montagu's harriers. Autumn is the best season to see migration, with huge numbers of geese, swans, ducks and waders passing through. Many of these stay for the winter and can also be seen from roads around other parts of the fjord.

Nissum Fjord

Nissum Fjord is situated north of Ringkøbing Fjord and is another excellent area for birdwatching. It lies roughly 60 miles (100km) north of Esbjerg and is best viewed from the coastal dune road that runs through Torsminde.

The fjord is a more or less landlocked freshwater lake that is the haunt of breeding waders and wildfowl in the spring and summer. Species to look for include black-tailed godwits, ruffs, avocets, garganeys and pintails.

In autumn, migrant geese and waders arrive here in their thousands and many stay during the winter. Pine forests to the south of the fjord are good for woodland birds.

Hansted Nature Reserve

This reserve lies between Klitmøller and Hanstholm on the North Sea coast, northwest of the Limfjord. The coast road runs along the western border of the reserve, and another road runs inland via Nors and close to the perimeter of Hansted.

The reserve is closed during the breeding season, but there is open access at other times of the year.

Habitats here are a mixture of sand dunes, heathland and lakes. One lake, Vandet Sø, can be seen particularly well from the road which runs inland from Klitmøller. Wetland birds breed on the reserve and large numbers of migrating geese,

Greylag Geese

Of the four species of grey geese regularly seen in Denmark, only the greylag breeds here. The other three – pink-footed, white-fronted and bean – are migrants and winter visitors to the country along with other greylags from further north in Europe. The greylag is the ancestor of the farmyard goose and can be recognised by its grey plumage and pink feet and bill. It is a heavily built bird, often nearly 36 inches (91cm) from bill to tail. It nests in marshy vegetation, building a nest of twigs and stems and lining it with down. When the young hatch they are soon taken to the water, where they find a degree of safety from land predators.

ducks and waders can be seen in spring and autumn.

Draved Skov Nature Reserve

There are wonderful, ancient woodlands in Draved Skov, which is the southwest corner of Jutland, roughly 43 miles (70km) south of Esbjerg. From the port, drive south to Løgumkloster and continue on the road south. The forest starts a few miles from here. There are waymarked trails, and a leaflet is available to assist visitors.

You will find an interesting mixture of tree species here, including small-leaved lime, oak and elm. In spring, look and listen for migrant breeding birds such as willow warblers, chiffchaffs, blackcaps and icterine warblers. Autumn is the best season for leaf colour and there is also an abundance of fungi on the woodland floor.

Rold Skov

Rold Skov (*skov* is Danish for forest) is the largest area of woodland in the country. In the northeast of Jutland, it is particularly interesting because of its mixture of tree species and the age structure of the forest as a whole. Within the forest there are areas of heathland, freshwater lakes and even some springs. The forest is best explored from the road which runs south from Aalborg to Hobro. South of Skørping, 15 miles (24km) south of Aalborg, is an excellent area which has open access and can be freely explored. **Rebild Bakker National Park**, just to the north of Skørping and within the

overall area of Rold Skov, is an attractive area with plenty of waymarked walks for the visitor. Leaflets in several languages are available to assist.

Spring is undoubtedly the best time of year here. You should hear and see songbirds such as icterine warblers, pied flycatchers and woodlarks, and birds of prey sometimes display overhead. Look out for buzzards, honey buzzards and goshawks.

Skallingen Nature Reserve

This reserve is sited on a sand dune peninsula some 12 miles (20km) west of Esbjerg, and is reached from Ho, east of Blåvand. The narrow strip of land has a sandy beach on the North Sea side, marshes on the landward side and dune flora over much of its area.

The marshes which face Esbjerg host large numbers of wading birds and wildfowl during migration times, in spring and particularly in autumn.

Rømø Nature Park

Rømø is an island off the west coast of Jutland, roughly 30 miles (50km) south of Esbjerg. It can be reached via a causeway that runs from Skærbæk to Lakolk. It is essentially a huge stabilised sandbank with a variety of habitats including saltmarsh, lakes and reed-beds.

It is good for birdwatching at any time of year. There are breeding wetland birds in the summer, wintering wildfowl and waders, and a wealth of migrant birds in spring and autumn.

Rands Fjord Nature Park

At one time this fjord was midway between Vejle and Fredericia on Jutland's east coast, connected with the sea, but it became landlocked in comparatively recent times and is now freshwater in nature. To reach the park, drive southeast from Vejle. Roughly fpur miles (6km) beyond Børkop, the road crosses the eastern edge of the park, just before you reach the village of Egeskov. Much of the area can be seen by exploring minor roads along the northern edge of the park – between Overhøl, Nebbegård and Østerskov – and to the south between Egeskov and Østerskov.

The fjord lake is important as a stop-off point for migrant waders and wildfowl, while the marshes and reed-beds harbour breeding birds such as reed warblers and bearded tits.

North Zealand

Using Copenhagen as a base, there are several excellent wildlife sites within easy reach of the city for those visitors with a car:

Calm water on Roskilde Fjord

Nekselø Nature Reserve is a small island sited on the northwest coast of Zealand, roughly 75 miles (120km) west of Copenhagen. Drive west from the city to Jyderup and then northwest to Havnsø, from where you can take a boat to the island. Visitors will find a mixture of meadows, valleys and lakes here. Meadow flowers are good in the spring and wetland birds breed here.

Roskilde Fjord is a beautiful fjord surrounded by attractive countryside, roughly 19 miles (30km) west of Copenhagen. Three parts of the southern end of the fjord have been designated Landscape Protection Areas. Roads run along both the eastern and western shores from Roskilde to Frederikssund and through Skibby and Skuldelev respectively. Along the shores, visitors will find freshwater lakes, beech woodlands and meadows, full of breeding birds in summer and migrant and wintering wildfowl and waders at other times of the year.

Hillerød lies 19 miles (30km) northwest of Copenhagen and is a central point for several sites of natural history interest. Just to the north of the town is the forest of Gribskov, one of Denmark's largest. The trees are a mixture of beech and pine. Waymarked walks and trails allow easy access, and visitors can look for woodland birds such as icterine warblers, nuthatches, pied flycatchers, buzzards and honey buzzards. One of the specialities of the area is the black woodpecker. On the eastern edge of the forest and between Hillerød and the town of Helsingør is a lake known as **Esrum Sø**. The area is a nature reserve, mainly because of its importance to wintering wildfowl, and footpaths allow for easy exploration. South of Hillerød is **Store Dyrehave** (the Great Deer Park), an area of open, park woodland.

Farum Nature Park is less than 12 miles (20km) from the outskirts of Copenhagen, northwest of the city. A network of footpaths allows visitors to explore the marshy ground and the three lakes within the park. Wetland birds and marsh flowers can be seen.

Southern Zealand and Adjacent Islands

As you travel south from Copenhagen, the scenery becomes increasingly rural. There are several areas of particular interest to the visitor: **Tystrup Nature Park** lies between Ringsted and Fuglebjerg in southwest Zealand. Lakes, marshes, woodland and meadows make up this reserve, which is good for breeding and wintering wildfowl and waterbirds.

Høje Møn Nature Park occupies the eastern tip of Møn, and has interesting chalk cliffs. **Ulvshale Nature Park** is the oldest in Denmark and occupies the northwestern tip of Møn. The peninsula can be reached from Keldbymagle and visitors will find woodland, heaths, meadows and wetlands.

Gedser, on the island of Falster, is the southernmost point of Denmark. Migrant birds are often concentrated here in spring, but more especially in autumn. Look for birds of prey, including sparrowhawks and honey buzzards.

Farmland Birds

Over the centuries, good use has been made of Denmark's lowland soils, and farmland is the country's most widespread habitat. Although wildlife is increasingly being edged out of the picture, a good many species are adaptable and live alongside people.

Arable fields harbour such hardy birds as rooks, pheasants and grey partridges while, near the coast, flocks of geese and ducks can sometimes be seen in autumn and winter.

Where meadows are left for haymaking, there is usually a rich and colourful flora. Small mammals abound, and predators such as kestrels and buzzards take advantage of their numbers.

FOOD AND DRINK

Practical

This section (with the yellow band) includes food, drink, shopping, accommodation, nightlife, tight budget, special events etc.

FOOD AND DRINK

There is little regional variation in Danish food and though it is not cheap, the quality is consistently high.

As Denmark is surrounded by the sea, it is not surprising that fish such as herring, plaice, salmon and shellfish feature widely on menus. Traditional fish dishes you should sample include *gravad laks* (salmon marinated in dill) served with a sweet mustard dressing, *jomfruhummer* (Norwegian crayfish), and *rødspættefilet remoulade* (fillet of plaice with remoulade sauce).

The choice of meat is usually limited to pork, beef and veal – lamb appears less frequently, and British visitors will be surprised not to find any bacon (the Danes export it all). Try *frikadeller* (pork meatballs served with a thick gravy), *fransk bøf* (fillet steak with parsley butter and chips), *mørbradbøf* (pork tenderloin with mushroom sauce) and *skipperlabskovs* (thick beef stew). *Biksemad* consists of meat, potatoes and fried onion,

and *medisterpølse* is a spiced pork sausage.

Popular puddings include *pandekager* (pancakes), *æblekage* (a type of apple cake) and *rødgrød* (red berry jelly), always generously laced with *fløde* (cream) or *flødeskum* (whipped cream). There is also a huge range of *is* (ice cream).

Specific to Denmark is *smørrebrød* (open sandwiches) – a slice of *rugbrød* (rye bread) with a generous topping of, perhaps, roast beef or pork, liver pâté, shrimps in mayonnaise, egg or cheese, always prettily decorated with salad.

Koldt bord (cold table) is a huge help-yourself buffet – once widely available, but now only served at Copenhagen station and a few large hotels. It has both cold food (herring, salads, shellfish, smoked fish, meats) and hot (soup, vegetables, stew), as well as cheese and desserts – all temptingly displayed. But resist the temptation to heap all the food on your plate together – follow local custom and take just a few items, starting with

FOOD AND DRINK

herring. Each time you come back for more food, take a clean plate.

Drink

Beer is very popular, and produced by the country's two main breweries, Carlsberg and Tuborg. It is sold mainly in pubs and bars, as well as in *bodegas* and cafés which serve wine too (imported and therefore expensive). Generally, cafés open in the morning, pubs may open from noon.

The drinking laws are less severe than in the rest of Scandinavia and alcohol can be bought in supermarkets. Most Danish beer is *pilsner* (lager), sold in third-litre bottles. *Lys pilsner* is the lightest; *fadøl* (draught lager) is stronger and sold in half-litre sizes; *luxøl* (*Eksport* or *Guldøl* brands) is yet stronger, and *elefantøl* is a very strong special beer.

The Danes produce their own potato-based schnapps called *akvavit*, which may be flavoured with dill or caraway and is typically drunk in a single gulp. Tea (*the*) and coffee (*kaffe*) are widely available. Coffee is served black, often in a jug to give two cups, with separate cream or milk.

All local water (*vand*) is perfectly drinkable.

Meals and Mealtimes

Hotel breakfasts (*morgenmad*) are usually large, help-yourself affairs to set you up for the day. They may include fruit juice, cereals, milk, yogurt, fruit, cheese, cold meats, liver pâté, bread, rolls, Danish pastries, jam and tea or coffee.

Lunch (*frokost*) can be anything from a snack to a full meal. Many eating places offer lunchtime bargains in the form of a *tilbud* (special), which is a reduced main course or *dagens ret* (dish of the day), a fixed-price main course with extras – starter, pudding, or a drink. These offers may only be available for a limited time, perhaps 11.30hrs to 14.30hrs, and the same meal will cost more in the evening.

Evening meals (*aftensmad*), usually start early – normally from 17.30hrs to 20.30hrs, though you can dine until 22.00hrs in larger towns.

Eating Out

In restaurants, meals are attractively presented, the portions are generous and there is frequently a children's menu (*børnemenu*) or children's dishes (*børneretter*). Menus are frequently translated into English and German. The restaurants recommended in this book are there because they serve predominantly Danish food, but you will also find many ethnic and fast food restaurants, especially in the cities.

Bistros, *bodegas* and cafés sell light, inexpensive meals and drinks, and there are self-service cafeterias, often located in supermarkets and department stores. *Konditorier* specialise in creamy pastries, cakes and drinks, while grillbars and *fiskerestauranter* (fish restaurants) are self-explanatory. *Pølsevogn* are kiosks, often found in town squares, selling fast food such as sausages and hamburgers.

Kros (inns), hotels and motels generally have a restaurant and while pubs concentrate on beer, they also sell snacks. DSB restaurants at railway stations are reliably good and usually offer a set three-course meal, fast food and special children's dishes.

Food Shops

Denmark is well supplied with supermarkets and there are several chains (Irma, Netto, Kvickly) where you can easily buy picnic food – pâté, cold meats, cheese, prepared salads (often with egg or fish) and yogurts. Fishmongers also sell salads and snacks. *Bageri* (baker's shops) are also open on Sunday mornings.

SHOPPING

Denmark is well known for its excellent design, and goods on sale are always attractively displayed, of a high quality and rather expensive. Beautiful glass, porcelain and silverware are world-famous, and there is some lovely jewellery, perhaps of gold and silver, inlaid with semi-precious stones, or items made from amber washed

ashore on Danish beaches. Furniture would be a bulky purchase, but it can be shipped.

As the country is small, most goods are available everywhere, but larger towns naturally offer a greater choice. There are few department stores. Fashion is a high export earner, and designer names are widely flaunted. Furs – if you can bring yourself to wear them – leather goods and heavy knitted sweaters can be good value. In summer, many clothes and shoe shops put racks outside with cheaper goods (*tilbud*).

Danes have deft fingers and many shops sell a wide range of wool, knitting patterns and needlecraft supplies. Ready-made cushion covers and wall-hangings make good presents. Table decorations, such as candle-holders and candles, on sale with matching paper napkins, are fun to buy.

Value Added Tax

VAT (called MOMS in Danish) is high, but you can save by going to one of 2,000 shops displaying a Europe Tax-free Shopping

Danish cuisine is rich and varied

ACCOMMODATION

logo. You have to spend a certain minimum amount before you are entitled to a refund, and this minimum depends where you live. For residents living outside Scandinavia and the EC the minimum is Dkr 600; Scandinavian residents must spend at least Dkr 1,200, and the minimum for EC residents is Dkr 4,700. To obtain a refund you must get copies of your tax-free receipt, which must be stamped at the customs point when you leave Denmark. Kastrup Airport gives a cash refund in most currencies. Otherwise, send your stamped receipt(s) to **Europe Tax-free Shopping Denmark**, Kastruplundgåde 22.1, DK-2770 Kastrup, and you will eventually either receive a cheque or get your credit card reimbursed; a small administrative charge is deducted.

ACCOMMODATION

Hotels

Denmark offers a wide choice of places to stay, from expensive hotels to campsites. Several hotel chains operate in Denmark and some issue

---

Big Little Denmark is an excellent publication produced by the Danish Tourist Board, which describes a wide range of the accommodation available. They also publish annually a list of hotels throughout the country, giving details of addresses, telephone numbers, prices and facilities.

---

vouchers offering discounts at certain times of the year. Inn cheques (*krocheck*) are slightly different, valid at nearly 70 independent inns who have formed a group and which offer discounts of from 10 to 25 per cent – write to **Dansk Kroferie**, Søndergade 31, DK-8700 Horsens. The Danish Family Hotel Group (**Danske Familie Hoteller**, DK-7300 Jelling), with 40 hotels dotted around the country, gives reductions between mid-June and mid-August to families of four sharing a room.

Strangely enough, the cost of some accommodation can be lower during the peak holiday months (June to August), particularly at hotels which normally cater for the business fraternity. Several of the more expensive hotels in Copenhagen also reduce their prices at weekends, Christmas and Easter.

Hotels are not graded, but are of a uniformly high standard and very clean. At the top end of the market are a few manor houses, elegant mansions often centuries old, which offer modern standards of accommodation and very good meals too. At the other end of the price scale are seamen's hotels, located at many ports (no longer only for sailors) which can be fairly basic, and mission hotels, which serve no alcohol.

Self-catering

Many Danes own a summer-house on the coast, on an island or tucked away in the country, which they let during the

summer. They may be simple
structures of wood, brick or
stone, and some are thatched.
Holiday companies rent out
summerhouses too, fully
furnished and equipped except
for towels and bed linen. The
summerhouses are in three
categories. The cheapest is
fairly basic, for four people,
with toilet; middle range ones
have a shower and refrigerator
and sleep six, and the most
expensive sleep eight and have
a dishwasher. Prices vary
according to the month – May
and September are
considerably cheaper than high
summer. This kind of
accommodation is best booked
in advance and addresses of
the relevant holiday companies
are given in the booklet, *Big
Little Denmark*. Information
about renting is also available
locally from agencies and
tourist offices. Another variation
is to stay at one of the holiday
centres which provide little
houses or apartments, usually
on the coast. These sleep from
two to eight people and are
likely to have television and a
washing machine. Again, you
supply your own towels and
linen. Some apartments have
kitchens, but there is a café and
a restaurant on site. The centres
offer many activities for
children, usually including a
swimming pool, table tennis,
billiards, sauna and a play area.

Farmhouse Holidays

This kind of accommodation is
very popular and offers two
choices: you can stay in the
farmhouse and eat with the
family (either just breakfast, or

*It is possible to rent cottages, or you
might consider a home-swap*

supper too), or you can stay in a
separate self-catering cottage
or flat. You can book through a
travel agent or the local tourist
office.

Private Accommodation

You can stay in Danish homes –
book through a local tourist
office, at the tourist board's
accommodation office in
Copenhagen, or through **Host
and Guest Service**, The Studio,
635 Kings Road, London SW6
2ES (tel: 071-731 5340).

Home Exchange

Another good idea for families
is to swap homes, complete
with the toys and bicycles.
More information from **Dansk
Boligbytte**, c/o Homelink
International, 84 Lees Gardens,
Maidenhead, Berks SL6 4NT.
(Remember Danish school
holidays are from late June until
early August).

Youth Hostels

Youth and Family Hostels
(Danmarks Vandrerhjem) – 110

of them – are dotted all over Denmark and represent very good value for money. There are three categories of bedroom: the best are two- to six-bedded rooms, with own shower and toilet; the same size rooms are also available without shower and toilet, but probably with a washbasin; the cheapest youth hostels have beds only.

A big breakfast is always available but evening meals depend on the whim of the warden. However, most hostels have a kitchen, usually with fridge, crockery and saucepans where you can cook your own food (take matches in case there is only gas).

Locations and types of building vary greatly. You are not expected to do a 'chore', apart from cleaning your room. For people travelling alone, especially cyclists, hostels are ideal and cost about a fifth, or less, of the price of a single hotel room. Out of season, individuals may be able to have a room to themselves for an extra cost.

Join the Youth Hostels Association in your own country before you set off, and buy a sheet sleeping bag – otherwise you will have to hire one each night. In Denmark, the address is **Landsforeningen Danmarks Vandrerhjem**, Vesterbrogåde 39, 1620 København V, and they publish an English edition of their hostels guide, with photos and maps. A list of hostels is also available from the Danish Tourist Board.

For information on camping and caravanning, see page 112.

CULTURE, ENTERTAINMENT AND NIGHTLIFE

Denmark is a sophisticated country, and this is evident in its approach to culture. Civic pride also plays its part in attracting visitors, with well maintained buildings and gardens, statues of local worthies or modern sculptures and fountains placed at strategic points. There is competition between local museums for the most lively presentation of their town's history, which often goes far back to prehistoric times. Throughout Denmark old buildings are being carefully restored, and there are a number of reconstructed villages. Much importance is placed on modern art, and numerous galleries, often privately owned, are open to the public.

The Danes love music, and classical concerts are performed in museums, manor houses and churches, as well as in large city concert halls.

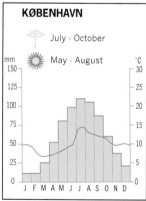

KØBENHAVN

July · October

May · August

WEATHER AND WHEN TO GO

The Royal Theatre, Copenhagen

Aalborg, Århus and Odense have their own symphony orchestras. Live jazz is very popular everywhere, and all over Denmark there are open-air concerts and music festivals in summer. Odense has an International Jazzhus. Street musicians swarm around pedestrianised streets, live bands play nightly in cafés, and discos can be heard full blast in many a bar.

Copenhagen has the most to offer – opera, ballet and theatre – although opera and ballet also flourish in Århus and Odense. Several towns have theatres, but most plays are performed in Danish. The capital also has the most varied nightlife, from expensive nightclubs, through live jazz to discos and gay bars, as well as the famous Tivoli Gardens.

In smaller towns and at coastal resorts there may be little alternative to discos in the evenings and perhaps a jazz band at weekends. There are many cinemas, which mainly show American films with Danish sub-titles. Television comes on in the early evenings and tends to be serious, but often shows English language films.

Gambling has recently been declared legal in Denmark and six hotels now offer American and French roulette and blackjack: SAS Scandinavia (Copenhagen), Marienlyst (Helsingør), H C Andersen (Odense), Munkebjerg (Vejle), Limfjordshotellet (Aalborg), Royal (Århus).

WEATHER AND WHEN TO GO

Denmark is such a small country that there is little variation in the weather from north to south, but the seas certainly influence the temperatures, making the west and north coasts more windy. In Copenhagen, July and August are the warmest months, but also the wettest; May, June and September are warm and drier; April is one of the driest months, with almost double the October's hours of sunshine, but it can be cold. In winter, it rains a little for about half the days each month, and there may be snow between December and February. At this time of year, daylight hours are short and so are some museum opening hours. Bornholm has the mildest climate, because of its mid-Baltic location, with considerably more hours of sunshine than Copenhagen. During the course of a day, the weather can change quickly from rain to sunshine – and back, and dull mornings often turn into bright and warm afternoons. The wind, particularly on the west coast of Jutland, can really be a force to be reckoned with – there is a reason for all those windmills! So whenever and wherever you go in Denmark, take a sweater, an umbrella, a windproof (or waterproof) jacket as well as flat shoes to make walking on cobblestones more comfortable. But don't forget your sunglasses either!

HOW TO BE A LOCAL

Danes are cheerful and relaxed people who like socialising and going to parties. Food and drink are taken seriously and at meals, often candle-lit, certain formalities should be observed. It is, for example, more polite to take several small helpings rather than one large one. Children are taught to thank their parents for the meal and guests should thank their hosts the next day. It is strange that in Danish, and other Scandinavian languages, there is no single word for please!

Chatting over a beer or throwing back a glass of schnapps – remember to say 'skål' – is still popular, but severe drink/drive laws have now curtailed this pastime. The standard of living is high, but so are the taxes which go to support nursery provision, senior citizens, single parents and the unemployed. The Danes' high level of social concern is reflected in the quality of homes provided for the elderly. It is a very tolerant society, which is evident in the experiment of Christiania, in Copenhagen, where a large group of social outcasts, many of whom were drug addicts, have now lived for over 20 years, without paying taxes. The Danes are fairly uninhibited, and early in any conversation with a new acquaintance, you are likely to be asked personal questions – about your age, religion, earnings or sex life.

They are a nation of sun worshippers, who have organised their school and working hours to run from 08.00hrs to 16.00hrs to take full advantage of the long summer days. Many families own or rent a summerhouse in the country or by the sea. Watersports, especially sailing and wind surfing, are very popular. Fitness is rated highly, as is cycling – not too demanding in this flattish country. Soccer is their favourite team sport, and they are also keen on badminton and golf.

A sound tradition of education exists in Denmark and English-speaking visitors will be delighted, but perhaps somewhat put to shame, by how well young Danes speak English.

There is a strong feeling of national identity and the Danish flag (Dannebrog) frequently flutters from flagpoles in town and city streets – and often in gardens for family celebrations. The Danes are sensible and rational in their dress (for comfort, not fashion) and behaviour (friendly but not overbearing), and so may appear rather serious to outsiders. Occasionally, however, delightful eccentricities emerge, such as a pipe-smoking woman, a couple wearing national costume, or the red-jacketed postman – and you will realise how wrong your first impressions were.

CHILDREN

The Danes have a tolerant attitude to children, and as Denmark is the home of Lego, many public places – airport lounges, shops, ferries, and some hotels – provide play areas, usually with piles of Lego bricks.

Parents are encouraged to bring children to Denmark through price reductions in hotels and in restaurants, which often serve special children's menus. At the seaside, shallow, sandy beaches (see **Beaches** in

the **Directory**) are ideal; holiday villages provide facilities such as a swimming pool, games rooms and play areas, and some special amusement parks offer lots of fun for children – and adults.

Sommerlands are large, attractive parks, with a single entrance fee covering all the activities. These may include trampolines, watercycles, rafts, ponies, motor go-carts, shooting galleries, volleyball, waterchutes, rowing boats and miniature golf. **Tivoli** are very much on the lines of the one in Copenhagen and you may have to pay for each ride.

Vandlands (or **Aqualands**) are a type of leisure centre offering an exciting range of water activities. The one in Aalborg is the biggest in northern Europe, with a large outdoor pool and bubble bath. Most of the attractions, however, are indoors where a series of pools, Turkish baths, saunas, jaccuzzis, swirl canals and water chutes are set in a tropical atmosphere. Most Vandlands have variations on this theme.

Museums, too, seem to make a special effort, bringing history to life by recreating old villages and encouraging Danish children to participate in activities such as living in an Iron Age village (in Lejre), or in a Viking festival (Århus). Many museums have toy displays.

Specially for Children
Aquaria: Denmarks Aquarium (Copenhagen); Nordsømuseet (Hirtshals); Saltvandsakvariet (Esbjerg); Funen Akvariet

(near Vissenbjerg); Nordsø Akvariet (Vorupør, near Thisted).

Aqualands (Vandlande): Bornholm, Gedser, Hanstholm, Lalandia, Odense, Sorø, and many sites throughout Jutland

Bird parks: Bregninge (Lolland); Jesperhus Blomsterpark (near Nykøbing, Mors); Frydenlund (at Tommerup).

Legoland: Billund.

Limestone mines (kalkgruber): Daugbjerg and Mønsted, both west of Viborg.

Old crafts: Hjerl Hede (Vinderup);Funen Village (Odense); Den Gamle Gård (Fåborg); the Old Town (Århus) and many others.

Open-air museums: Den Gamle By (Århus); Hjerl Hede (Vinderup); Funen Village (Odense); Sorgenfri (Lyngby, near Copenhagen).

Safari parks: Knuthenborg (Maribo, Lolland); Løveparken (Givskud).

Santaworld: Ringsted

Sommerlands: Djurs (Nimtofte)

Many attractions cater for children

with Aqualand and Science Centre; Falster (Bøtø); Fårup, Aquapark (Saltum, northeast of Blokhus); Funen (Årup); Mini-landsbyen (Rømø); Syd (Tinglev and Hee, near Ringkøbing); Zealand (Nykøbing S).

Tivoli: Copenhagen; Odense; Aalborg; Århus.

Toy collections: Vendsyssel (at Hjørring); Funen (Millinge); Viebæltegård (Svendborg).

Steam trains: Aalborg Station (on Limfjord Line); Mariager to Handest; Maribo to Bandholm (Lolland); Odense (DSB Railway Museum). Other steam railways are: Bryup–Vrads, Vejle–Jelling, Odder–Århus, Randers–Mariager (all on Jutland).

TIGHT BUDGET

Denmark, like the rest of Scandinavia, has a reputation for being one of the most expensive countries in Europe, and it is true that extras which most holidaymakers expect to enjoy – such as coffees, cakes, ice creams and drinks – may cost more than you thought.

The two cheapest ways of visiting Denmark are bringing your car (full) and self catering, or cycling round and staying at youth hostels, which are available to older people and families too. It is possible to stay at youth hostels and use public transport, but careful planning is essential because some hostels are a long way from the nearest public transport.

Budget Tips
• plan your trip to coincide with discount air fares
• if you are taking your car, look for bargain fares offered by Scandinavian Seaways
• if planning to hire a car, it is often cheaper to book in advance in your own country
• if you are self-catering, bring all the basics with you, such as tea, coffee, cereals and jams
• supermarkets in towns offer best value food shopping, but look also at fruit and vegetable stalls in street markets
• if eating out, bistros and cafés sell light, inexpensive meals, and there are self-service cafeterias, often located in supermarkets and department stores; have your main meal at lunchtime, when set-price meals and other bargains are often available (see page 96)
• if you like the occasional drink, bring in the maximum amount of alcohol permitted for your own consumption
• travel cards issued by certain towns can be money savers
• family groups looking for accommodation should ask about the availability of family rooms (see also **Accommodation**, page 98).

SPECIAL EVENTS

It would seem that there is little time for work in Denmark in summer with all that is going on – town and music festivals, markets and fairs, concerts, sporting events, exhibitions and anniversaries. Many towns hold weekly jazz concerts and some churches and castles, such as Spøttrup (Balling) and Kolding have classical music concerts. Trotting races are held in Copenhagen, Århus and some other towns, and regattas and fishing contests take place everywhere. Tilting contests and animal fairs are regularly held in South Jutland, and Midsummer's Eve (23 June) is celelebrated throughout Denmark with bonfires and local entertainment.
The Danish Tourist Board publishes a 60-page booklet, *Coming Events*, listing all activities between April and the end of September, as well as a guide for October to March. A separate leaflet, *Danish Music Festivals*, is produced by the Danish Music Information Centre (48 Vimmelskaftet, DK-1161 Copenhagen K). A selection of events is given below; most last for a day or weekend unless otherwise stated:

April
Løgumkloster: Spring Fair
Viborg: Horse and Junk Fair

May
Assens: Harbour Festival
Copenhagen: Carnival
Middelfart: Little Belt Jazz
  Festival

SPORT

Nyborg: Whitsun Fair
Nykøbing Mors: Pearl Festival
Ribe: Tulip Festival
Aalborg: Festival (one week)

June
Fåborg: Festival
Karrebæksminde: Jazz Festival
Odense: Funen Agricultural Show
Odense: Harbour Festival
Ringe: Midtfyns (Central Funen Festival – rock and folk)
Roskilde: Agricultural Show
Roskilde: Festival (rock, theatre, fair)
Silkeborg: Riverboat Jazz Festival
Skagen: Festival (folk and rock)
Sønderborg: Shooting Festival
Aalborg: Jazz Festival

July
Bornholm: Herring Festival (four days)
Bornholm: Music Festival (until first week September)
Copenhagen: Summer Festival (classical music – until mid-August)
Copenhagen: Jazz Festival (one week)
Fredericia: Jazz Festival
Maribo: Jazz Festival
Samsø : Festival (jazz and folk)
Skørping and Aalborg: Rebild Festival (4 July)

A recent scheme introduced in Copenhagen enables visitors to have free use of *bycykler* (city bikes) at several points in the city. You place a coin into the bike and the money is automatically returned when the bike is put back in the stand.

Sønderborg: Tilting Festival
Ærø: Grolle Festival
Åbenrå: County Tilting Festival (including Tattoo)
Århus: International Jazz Festival (one week)
Århus: Viking Meet

August
Dragør: Ullerup Junk and Horse Fair
Ebeltoft: Festival (music)
Esbjerg: North Sea Days
Fåborg: Harbour Festival
Randers: Festival (10 days, including Regatta)
Roskilde: Viking Fair
Silkeborg: Grand Prix Denmark (motor races)
Skanderborg: Danmarks Smukkeste (most beautiful rock) Festival
Tønder: Folk Festival
Viborg: Jazz Festival
Århus: Harbour Festival

September
Højer: Sheep Fair
Næstved: Troll Festival (one week)
Skanderborg: Tour de Gudenaa (canoe races)
Århus: Festival and Old-world Fair (nine days)

SPORT

The Danes are keen on sport, and tourists can participate in many activities. The Danish Tourist Board publishes a series of excellent booklets in several languages on all the sports listed below, and there are also facilities for boating (rowing boats), canoeing, go-karting, horse riding and walking. The local tourist offices can provide more information.

Cycling

The flat landscape makes Denmark particularly well suited to cycling and there are many cycle tracks in and between towns, as well as marked cycle routes. Visitors can easily share this activity either by bringing their own bike or hiring one from a local cycle shop, youth hostel or tourist office at a daily or weekly rate. You must pay a deposit and return the machine to the original hirer.

Bicycles can also be hired at some railway stations and be taken on most trains. A leaflet (in Danish) *Cycler i tog* (bicycles by train) gives information about prices and timetables. Cycles can be taken on other forms of transport too, including domestic flights, but not on city buses.

The Danish Tourist Board produces a very useful map, *On a Bike in Denmark*, showing cycling tracks and marked routes, and giving information about cycling holidays. On cycling package holidays you get a discount if you bring your own bike, and sometimes your luggage can be transported separately for you. Many local tourist offices also publish maps for cyclists, avoiding main roads.

In Jutland particularly, the winds can be strong and you will find journeys from west to east easier (and quicker) than those from east to west!

Dansk Cyklist Forbund

(Danish Cyclists Federation), Rømersgåde 7, 1362 København, (tel: 33 32 31 21) can give you more information.

Windmills are part of the landscape

Fishing

Denmark is a fisherman's paradise, but you need to bring your own rod and line. For saltwater fishing (herring, cod and flatfish) you do not need a licence, and you can fish from harbours or piers and from almost anywhere along the coast. Deep sea fishing trips with local fishermen can also be arranged.

For fresh-water fishing (trout, eel, salmon), you need a licence from the local angling association – ask at the local tourist office. You will also have to pay a fee, for a day or for a number of hours. 'Put and take' is very popular, where local lakes are specially stocked with fish. Certain restrictions are in force regarding fishing near river mouths.

If you want to bring your own maggots, check with the airline first (the ferries accepts them, sealed). Otherwise you will have to dig for Danish worms. Package fishing holidays are available, in hotels or self-catering accommodation, and the fishing licence is included in the price.

Golf

There are 70 courses in Denmark, and almost as many on Zealand as on the whole of Jutland. Most are 18-hole courses, and you can hire clubs and a trolley on a daily basis. To play on any course you need to show the membership card of a recognised golf club.

The leaflet *Danish Inn Holidays* lists all the courses; some of the inns offer complimentary or reduced-price green fees. You can buy a golf package holiday which may include green fees.

Sailing

Danish yachting enthusiasts are fortunate that their country is composed of so many islands, which provides such excellent and varied sailing. The most attractive areas are around Funen, where there are over 100 islands, and the Limfjord area. As well as the numerous harbours, a number of new marinas have been constructed.

For overseas visitors, however, it is not so easy. Swedes,

Germans and the Dutch can sail their own boats to Denmark, but visitors from further afield will have to tow their own boats overland. Smaller yachts can be taken on the ferry to Esbjerg. For boat hire, contact **Dansk Sejlunion**, Idrættens Hus, DK-2605 Brøndby (tel: 42 45 55 55). One company which hires out yachts is **Nordia Boat Charter**, Vester Alle 50, Hammerum, DK-7400 Herning.

It may be possible to hire a yacht for a few days, but you will need to show a certificate of competence. Package holidays for people who want to learn to sail are based at Svendborg, Skive, Rudkøbing and Rungsted Kyst.

Swimming

Apart from the sea (see **Beaches** in the **Directory**), most towns have a swimming pool and some also have an Aqualand (see **Children**). A slightly unusual version is **Søhøjlandet Centre** at Gjern, northwest of Århus, which offers a range of other sports too – riding, squash and tennis.

Windsurfing

The best areas for experienced surfers are along the northwest coasts of Jutland and Zealand, the north and west coasts of Funen and around the islands of Møn, Falster, Langeland and Bornholm. Many centres offer instruction in surfing: these are mostly located on the east coasts of Jutland and Zealand. Even if you are not undergoing instruction, several places hire out surfboards. Maps are published which grade the areas according to difficulty.

Directory

This section (with the biscuit-coloured band) contains day-to-day information, including travel, health and documentation.

Contents

Arriving

By Air
Denmark does not have its own national airline but has a share in **SAS**, the Scandanavian Airlines System, which operates flights to Copenhagen (Kastrup Airport) from about 70 different countries. About 40 other foreign airlines also fly in to Copenhagen. Two Danish carriers are **Maersk** (in London tel: 071-734 4020), which flies to Billund from London Gatwick, Brussels, Amsterdam and Stockholm; and **Danair**, an SAS subsidiary which flies within Denmark (contact SAS in London, tel: 071-638 7920). Apart from Copenhagen, other Danish airports which receive international flights are Aalborg

Danish postboxes have a distinctive rounded top and bright red livery

DIRECTORY

Denmark is a seafaring nation

(flights from Kristiansand and Gothenborg); Billund (see above); Århus (flights from London Heathrow, Malmø, Oslo and Stavanger), and Esbjerg (flights from Aberdeen, Dundee and Humberside).

Flight time from London to Copenhagen is under two hours. Flights also go to Copenhagen from Aberdeen, Birmingham, Dublin, Glasgow and Manchester.

Kastrup airport is large and modern with excellent shops, including duty-free; it is six miles (10km) southeast of Copenhagen, with a frequent bus service to Copenhagen Central station. Billund airport is smaller, just over a mile (2km) from the town and within walking distance of Legoland. Århus airport (Tirstrup) also operates a bus service to Århus bus station, 22 miles (35km) away. Esbjerg airport is six miles (10km) northeast of Esbjerg, just off the E20.

A list of scheduled flight operators to Denmark is in the Danish Tourist Board's brochure *Big Little Denmark*.

Several airlines, including SAS and Maersk, reduce their fares in the summer months, when fewer business travellers fly.

By Rail

Trains run direct to Denmark from Germany, crossing the border at Padborg and Rødby (by ferry). International through trains operate from Sweden, Norway and Britain via ferries (see below). Inter-Rail tickets are valid in Denmark.

By Ferry

Denmark has numerous ferry connections with other north European countries; these can transport cars, caravans and bicycles. **Scandinavian Seaways** (in Britain, tel: 081-205 0500 for a brochure; 0255 241234 to make a booking) operates two services from England to Esbjerg, each taking about 20 hours. From Harwich there are three to four sailings a week, all year, and from Newcastle two sailings a week from mid-June to mid-August only, with a connecting boat-

train service to Copenhagen.
There are many crossings from
Germany, Sweden and Norway
and a few from Poland – details
can be found in the *Ferry Guide*
published by the Danish Tourist
Board.
Some ferry companies offer
discounts at certain times of the
year, and circular tour tickets
may be available on domestic
and international routes.
Further information about
ferries is available from the
Danish Tourist Board and
national motoring organisations.

By Road
The motorway border crossing
between Germany and
Denmark is at Frøslev; there
are other road crossings at
Kruså and Sæd, while minor
crossings at Rudbøl, Oksevejen
and Skomagerhus are open
infrequently. Other crossing

*Timetables for the ferries, buses
and trains are coordinated*

points can only be used by
Germans visiting Denmark.
Two coach companies run trips
from Britain to Denmark, each
cooperating with a ferry
company. **London Coaches**
(tel: 071-918 3456), with Olau
Line, goes three times a week
using the Sheerness to
Vlissingen crossing, while
Roundabout Enterprises (tel:
0923 835696) goes weekly with
Sally Ferries, using the
Ramsgate to Dunkerque route.
Both companies travel from
London to Copenhagen via
Fredericia, Århus and Odense.

Entry Formalities
Visitors, except Scandinavians,
need a national identity card or
passport, but no entry visa, for
stays of up to 90 days.
However, holders of a British
passport issued before 1
January 1983 may need a visa if
they were not born in the UK. A
British Visitor's Passport is
acceptable.

DIRECTORY

Beaches

Denmark's coastline, including all its islands, totals about 4,600 miles (7,400km), which means a lot of beaches. Most are sandy and backed by dunes. Few are 'developed' in the Mediterranean sense, but many have basic facilities. The wide, white beaches on the west coast of Jutland form one of the longest stretches of sand – at Blokhus, for example, cars can be driven on to the beach. This coast does face the North Sea, though, which can make it cold, rough and windy. Calmer conditions and shallower waters prevail on Jutland's east coast, and on the east coasts of Funen, Falster and Langeland. The most pleasant of Zealand's beaches are on the north and southwest coasts – this section boasts 11 **Blue Flags**, awarded by the EC for clean and unpoluted beaches, along 40 miles (65km). Other islands with lovely beaches include Fanø and Bornholm; few beaches are rocky, and dunes in north and west Jutland make varied coastal contours. The keen-eyed may find fossils (on Mørs or Fur), and look out for amber. Bathing is prohibited at a few harbours, identified by the flying of danger flags. Topless bathing is allowed on all, and nude bathing on many beaches.

Camping and Caravanning

There are about 500 campsites in Denmark, in the countryside and on the coast. All the sites are classified and given star ratings from one to three. One-star sites provide minimum sanitary installations and drinking water; two-star sites have showers, shaving points, laundry and ironing facilities, while three-star sites have even higher standards. The price depends on the classification. Many sites are well laid out in pleasant locations. Some have shops, a few have pools. Spending the night in a car, tent, dormobile or mobile home on land outside an official site without the landowner's permission is forbidden, as is camping in car parks or laybys – and people parking on sand dunes or beaches are fined on the spot. Foreign visitors should get an **International Camping Carnet** before they leave home. Otherwise, they can buy a pass at their first site, which is valid for all approved campsites in Denmark. The Danish Tourist Board publishes a free leaflet which lists all sites and their ratings. Further information and the official guide to sites, *Camping Danmark,* can be obtained from **Campingrådet**, Hesseløgade 16, DK-2100 København Ø. Many Danish campsites have static caravans or cabins for rent, usually available only on a weekly basis, from a Saturday. They are normally fully equipped except for bed linen.

Chemists see Pharmacies

Crime

Denmark is a very safe country, but you should not take any risks. When parking your car, make sure that it is locked and that no valuables or luggage are visible. It is unwise to

Pleasure craft from the humblest...

wander around Christiania, in Copenhagen, at night, but the rest of the city and other large towns are perfectly safe.

Customs Regulations
Visitors can bring in cars, motorcycles, caravans and boats, free of duty, but they must not lend them to Danish residents nor accept payment for transporting people in them. All personal articles can also be imported duty-free. It is forbidden to import fresh, frozen or smoked meat or meat products, but tinned meat for your own consumption is permitted.
Apart from the usual restrictions on the importation of tobacco, alcohol and perfume by people aged 17 and over, Denmark also has strict rules about importing coffee and tea. Coffee can only be imported by

those aged 15 and over, but children may import tea, perfume and *eau de toilette*. There are no restrictions on the import or export of Danish or foreign currency.

Disabled Travellers
Denmark's provision for the handicapped is excellent. The Danish Tourist Board publishes a comprehensive booklet *Access in Denmark – a travel guide for the disabled* which gives a comprehensive list of accessible places and facilities for wheelchair users, including facilities on trains, ferries and at airports, public toilets, accommodation, and parking distances from museums.

Driving
Driving in Denmark is a pleasure as the roads are well maintained and traffic is light. Drivers who want to go on more scenic routes should

DIRECTORY

follow the new **Marguerit-rute** (Marguerite Route), over 2,000 miles (3,500km) of roads, following the road signs which feature a yellow flower on a brown background. Maps are on sale at tourist offices and Statoil service stations.

Some points to watch are that road signs indicating places on the left are occasionally set on the lefthand side of the road, and only at the junction itself, not in advance. Motorways, which are toll-free, are often only two lanes in each direction, and have few service stations. Be careful when turning right in towns as a cycle track often runs between the pavement and the road; drivers must give way to cyclists who may be going straight on.

The minimum age for drivers is 18. Foreign cars must display a nationality plate and carry a warning triangle. (See also **Documents**, opposite.)

Accidents and breakdowns
If you have an accident, phone 112 for the emergency services. Accidents must be reported to the **Dansk Forening for International Motorkøretøjsforsikring**, Amaliegade 10, DK-1256 København K (tel: 33 13 75 55). If you break down, get the phone number of the nearest **Falck** from the phone book; emergency phones are installed on motorways. Both operate a 24-hour service, for which you will have to pay. If your car cannot be fixed on the spot it will be towed to a garage, but if you can get your

...to the highest can be seen here

car to a garage yourself, do so. You will have to pay VAT (currently 25 per cent) for materials and labour on the repair. (See also **Motoring Organisations**, below.)

Alcohol
There are strict penalties for motorists who drink and drive and it is therefore advisable not to do so.

Car rental
This is widely available from large international or smaller local companies, but it can be cheaper to book it in advance in your own country. By law you must be 20 years old to hire a car, but some companies do not accept drivers under 25.

Documents
For driving your own car, you will need to take your (valid) driving licence and the car's registration papers. A Green Card is not compulsory, but is recommended, and you should take out extra insurance.

Fuel
Petrol is sold in litres, often in self-service garages (*tank selv* or *selvbetjening*). There are two grades of leaded – leaded (super benzin) 98 octane, and low-lead 96 octane – and three of unleaded (*blyfri*), sold in 92, 95 and 98 octanes. There are plenty of garages in Denmark but few on motorways. Some garages accept credit cards, and at some automatic pumps you feed in kroner notes (Dkr 50 and 100).

Lights
It is now compulsory to use dipped headlamps at all times, even during daylight hours. The lights of Danish-registered cars are of a lower density than UK-registered vehicles, so drivers should dip their lights early on meeting oncoming vehicles. All drivers with assymetric headlights, such as on right-hand drive cars, must cover part of the glass of the headlamp with an opaque material or use beam deflectors, available from motorist shops or motoring organisations.

Motorcycles
Riders and passengers must wear a helmet, and use dipped headlights always.

Motoring Organisations
Forenede Danske Motorjere – **FDM** (the Danish Motoring Organisation) does not provide a breakdown service, but offers legal and technical help to members of motoring organisations such as the British AA, which are affiliated to AIT (Alliance Internationale de Tourism). Their head office is at Firskovvej 32, PO Box 500, DK-2800 Lyngby (tel: 45 93 08 00).

Parking
In some towns with a car park you have to buy a parking ticket and display it: *parkeringsbillet påkrævet* means that a pay-and-display ticket is compulsory. In other towns, parking is free but you must display a parking disc which resembles a clock, and you set the hands to the nearest quarter-hour following your arrival time. Signs such as *1 time*, *2 timer* mean that you can park for one or two hours. Discs are available from tourist

DIRECTORY

offices, FDM (motoring organisation) offices, garages, post offices and police stations and some banks.

Parkering forbudt means no parking, though you are allowed three minutes to pick up or drop off passengers. Parking metres must be fed on weekdays (09.00–18.00hrs) and Saturdays (09.00–13.00hrs). *Stopforbud* means no stopping.

Seat belts
It is compulsory for drivers and passengers over 15 years of age to wear seat belts if they are fitted.

Speed limits
On motorways the maximum speed is 110km/h (69mph); other roads 80km/h (50mph) and in built-up areas 50km/h (31mph). The maximum speed on motorways for cars towing a caravan or trailer is 70km/h (44mph).

Traffic regulations
Drive on the right, overtake on the left. Most signs are international, but when you emerge from a side road on to a main road there is often a line of white triangles (sharks' teeth) painted on the surface: this means that the traffic on the main road has right of way. You must not turn right at red lights unless a green arrow shows.

For several offences, including speeding or careless driving, you can be fined on the spot (although as a visitor, your licence will not be endorsed) and if you cannot pay, your car may be impounded.

Electricity
The electric current is 220 volts AC (50Hz) and sockets are of the two-point Continental type. You will need an adaptor for appliances from the UK and a voltage transformer for appliances from the US or Canada.

Embassies and Consulates
United Kingdom
Embassy
40 Kastelsvej,
DK-2100 København
tel: 35 26 46 00

Consulates
Esbjerg, Fredericia, Herning, Odense, Rønne (Bornholm), Åbenra, Aalborg and Århus.

Australia
Embassy
21 Kristianiagade,
DK-2100 København
tel: 35 26 22 44

Canada
Embassy
1 Kristen Bernikowsgåde,
DK-1105 København K
tel: 33 12 22 99

Republic of Ireland
Embassy
Østbanegade 21
DK-2100 København
tel: 31 42 32 33

USA
Embassy
24 Dag Hammarskjölds Alle,
DK-2100 København
tel: 31 42 31 44

Emergency Telephone Numbers
Dial 112 for police, fire or ambulance services. Emergency calls are free from public telephone boxes.

Entertainment

For big cities, the most up-to-date information is in *Copenhagen This Week* and *Århus This Week*, both published monthly and available free from tourist offices, hotels and airports. Many other towns produce leaflets about local events, available from the same places.

Health

In the case of sudden illness or an accident, all visitors are entitled to free medical treatment in hospital. If you need a doctor for a non-urgent case ask your hotel or campsite warden to phone for you: an answer-phone service refers callers to a 'doctor on duty' service and each town has its own phone number.

Health insurance is not necessary for some categories of EC visitors – employees, self-employed people and pensioners – as they are automatically insured in Insurance Group 1 which entitles them to free medical care and a refund of part of any charges made by dentists and chemists. Other British nationals are covered by Insurance Group 2 which gives them a smaller refund.

British citizens should get booklet **T2**, *Health Advice for Travellers Inside the European Community,* from post offices. Fill in both forms at the back of the leaflet and get them stamped at a post office, then take form E111 with you to Denmark. If you do receive medical treatment and the Danish doctor insists on cash,

Entertainment may be innovative

ask for a receipt and take it with your E111 to the local health office in Denmark (Kommunens social-og sundhedsforvaltning). (See also **Pharmacies**)

Tap water is safe to drink throughout Denmark.

Holidays

On these days, all banks, businesses and shops are closed: New Year's Day, Maunday Thursday, Good Friday, Easter Monday, Great Prayer Day (fourth Friday after Good Friday), Ascension Day, Whit Monday, Constitution Day (5 June, from noon), Christmas Day, Boxing Day. School summer holidays run approximately between 20 June and 20 August.

Lost Property

In Copenhagen you can try the following phone numbers, depending on where you lost your belongings: **aeroplane** – tel: 31 50 32 11 (from 10.00hrs to noon only); **bus** – tel:36 45 45 45; **train** – tel:36 44 20 10; **police** – tel: 31 74 88 22.

For lost **credit cards**, tel: 44 89 25 00; American Express tel: 80 01 00 21.
For the **local police** in Copenhagen, tel: 33 14 14 48; in Århus, tel: 86 13 30 00; in Aalborg, tel: 98 12 62 00.

Media
Radio Denmark broadcasts a five-minute English news bulletin at 08.10hrs, Monday to Friday, on Programme 1 (90.8MHz). English newspapers are on sale in Copenhagen and other large towns.

The white cliffs of Møn

Money Matters
The currency is the Danish Krone (Dkr), made up of 100 øre. Kroner come in notes of 50, 100, 500 and 1,000, and in coins of 1, 5, 10, and 20; there are also coins of 25 and 50 øre. Travellers' cheques and Euro-cheques can be exchanged for Danish currency. There are also cash machines (called *Kontanten*) in Copenhagen and elsewhere which will give you Danish currency if you insert a Visa or Eurocheque card. Banks charge a flat rate of commission for exchanging travellers' cheques and foreign

currency, which may be very high and differs from bank to bank. Danish banks may refuse to exchange foreign bank notes of high denominations.
Credit cards (Mastercard, Visa) and charge cards (American Express and Diners) are widely accepted in shops, restaurants, hotels and garages in large towns, but may not be accepted in rural areas.

Opening Times

Banks
Open Monday to Friday only, 09.30-16.00hrs; on Thursdays open until 18.00hrs, though this can vary outside Copenhagen. In Copenhagen, outside banking hours, you can change money at the main railway station (06.45–22hrs mid-April to September; 07.00–21.00hrs October to mid-April), at Tivoli (noon to 23.00hrs) and at the airport (06.30–22.00hrs); in Århus, at department stores Magasin and Salling; at the tourist office in Aalborg.

Shops
Shopping hours vary from town to town. Shops in Copenhagen open Monday to Saturday 10.00hrs, and close 17.30hrs (19.00hrs or 20.00hrs Friday and 13.00hrs or 14.00hrs on Saturdays). In July and August shops on Strøget may be open on Saturday and Sunday afternoons.
In most other towns, shops open Monday to Saturday, any time between 09.00 and 10.00hrs and close at 17.30hrs, except on Friday, when they stay open to 19.00 or 20.00hrs, and Saturday, when they stay

open until around 13.00hrs. On the first Saturday each month all shops can stay open in the afternoon. On Sunday mornings, bakeries and sweet shops open.

Museums, Churches, etc
If you want to see a particular museum, check the opening times with the tourist office or museum itself. In Copenhagen and many other towns, most museums are open on Sundays and closed on Mondays.
The story is different, however, with more seasonal outdoor entertainment. **Tivoli**, for example, is open from the last week in April until mid-September (daily 10.00hrs until midnight), while **Legoland** opens from 1 May until the third Sunday in September (daily 10.00–20.00hrs, or to 21.00hrs in high season). Some outdoor museums stay open for longer hours during the summer. Manor houses may be open in summer months only and perhaps on certain days. Churches are open for some hours most days, but may not welcome sightseers on Sundays.

Tourist Offices
In Copenhagen, June to mid-September from 09.00–18.00hrs every day; in May, Monday to Friday, 09.00–17.00hrs, Saturday until 14.00hrs and Sunday until 13.00hrs. For the rest of the year, Monday to Friday 09.00–17.00hrs and Saturday until noon. Times vary in other cities, and many tourist offices stay open longer in summer.

Pharmacies

The *Apotek* (chemist's shop) usually occupies a prime site in town, often in an old building in the main square. Generally their opening hours are the same as other shops, but those in larger cities may stay open 24 hours a day.

Pharmacies are the only places which sell medicines. If you regularly take a prescribed medicine, make sure you do not run out of it while you are in Denmark as chemists dispense prescriptions from Scandinavian doctors only. Preparations which are readily available over the counter in the UK may be on prescription only in Denmark.

Information leaflets issued by local tourist offices often carry the address and phone number of the pharmacy. (See also **Health**)

Personal Safety

Always make sure your money, passport and travel documents are safe – in your hotel, on your person or in your car. (See also **Crime**)

Places of Worship

The state religion is Protestant, and church services are held on Sundays. Some Copenhagen churches, including St Alban, the Pentecostal Church and the International Baptist Church, hold services in English. Buddhists, German Evangelicals, Jehovah's Witnesses, Jews, Muslims, Quakers, Roman Catholics and Seventh Day Adventists will all find places of worship in Copenhagen. More information from *Copenhagen This Week*. In the rest of the country, Protestantism prevails.

Post Offices

In general, post offices open daily (except Sunday) from 09.00hrs or 10.00–17.00hrs. On Saturday those that open at all close at about noon. The post office at Copenhagen Central railway station opens daily on weekdays 08.00–22.00hrs, Saturday 09.00–16.00hrs, and Sunday 10.00–17.00hrs.

Public Transport

Denmark has an efficient and punctual public transport system of trains, buses and ferries. All the timetables are sensibly coordinated so that no vehicle departs until the expected one arrives.

Air

Copenhagen is not only the hub of international routes, but also of domestic ones, operated by **Danair**, which flies to nine towns on Jutland, as well as to Odense and to Bornholm. From Roskilde an air taxi flies to some of the islands (Anholt, Læsø, Samsø, Ærø). Information about internal flights is available from Danair (not to be confused with the British charter company, Dan-air) by telephoning SAS or Maersk (see page 109).

Rail

The state railway system (**DSB** – Danske Statsbaner) operates most trains, but some lines are still privately run (the one to Skagen, for example) and do not accept all tickets, including Inter-rail and Nordturist. *IC3 tog* (express trains) provide fast and comfortable long-distance travel throughout the country, but their coverage is somewhat limited.

Newspapers, refreshments and payphones are available; seats (first and second class) must be reserved.

Intercity trains run more frequently, often running an hourly service between main towns. Reservations are compulsory on trains crossing the Great Belt.

The country is divided into zones, and ticket prices are based on the distance travelled; for longer journeys the cost per zone is reduced. Passengers travelling (second class) 13 zones or more (approximately 62 miles/100km) may be eligible for reductions, such as children (aged 4 to 11), young people aged 12 to 25 and students, three or more adults travelling together. There are even greater savings for seven or more adults travelling together, providing the reservation was made by 15.00hrs on the day before the journey.

Children under the age of four go free at all times.

(See also **Senior Citizens** and

Student and Youth Travel, page 122)

Cheap travel is available on Tuesdays, Wednesdays and Thursdays. Tickets can be bought on the train but cost more. A strip of 10 tickets (*10-tursklippekort*) is also cheaper, but probably not much use to tourists. Free local timetables are available at stations and at tourist offices.

There are luggage trolleys at some stations, for which a charge may be made (a lock system operates at Copenhagen's main station, for which you currently require a Dkr10 coin) but is refundable when the trolley is returned. Left luggage offices exist at some stations.

In the metropolitan (HT) area around Copenhagen a separate, integrated transport system operates, covering both trains and buses. The trains are called S-trains and the main station is København H. (See **Transport**, and **Copenhagen Card** on page 26)

The graceful curve of the longboat is reflected in the longhouse

Model ships hang in many of Denmark's churches

Buses

Not many long-distance buses operate in Denmark, but the fares are lower than on trains. Buses are the only option in Funen and northeast Jutland. Local buses are modern and comfortable. Each town sets its own basic ticket price, and the more tickets you buy, the less each journey costs. Some towns offer special rates to tourists, notably Odense, Aarlborg and Århus.

Ferries

Over 90 different ferry services sail from Danish harbours, more frequently in summer than in winter. If you have a car, the cost of your journey depends on the number of passengers; foot passengers pay less. If your train or bus journey includes a ferry crossing, this is covered in the ticket price. On busy routes (the Great Belt ferry and Rødby to Puttgarden) and on summer weekends, it is sensible to book in advance. The Danish Tourist Board publishes a Ferry Guide (*Ferjer*) giving fares and frequency of sailings on routes

in Denmark and to Germany, Norway, Sweden and the UK.

Senior Citizens

Men and women who receive an old age pension in their own country are entitled to reduced train fares in Denmark on production of their passport and senior citizens' travel card. British travellers aged 60 and over, whether or not they have retired, are eligible for a 30 per cent discount on train fares in Denmark. To qualify, you must first buy a Senior Railcard in the UK, and then purchase a **Rail Europe Senior Card** which must be produced when buying a Danish train ticket.

Student and Youth Travel

Some reduced train fares are available (see **Rail** travel, above) for young people aged 12 to 25, and for students, through **DIS**, the Danish student travel organisation.
At the main railway station in Copenhagen, the **Inter-Rail Centre** offers the younger traveller information, a free shower, plus the chance to meet fellow travellers (open daily 07.00hrs to midnight, June to September). Accommodation in summer is provided at two Inter-Rail Points: at 19 Store Kannikestræde (tel: 33 11 30 31), and 15 Valdemarsgåde (tel: 31 31 15 74).
In Copenhagen the **Use It Youth Information Centre** (13 Rådhusstræde, tel: 33 15 65 18) is open daily from mid-June to mid-September, 09.00–19.00hrs (rest of year Monday to Friday, 10.00–16.00hrs), to help young people find cheap

accommodation and restaurants. Use It sorts out young people's travel problems, stores luggage (free), and makes contact between drivers and hitch-hikers leaving Copenhagen. It also provides information about the city, and publishes (in English) *Playtime* once a year and *Use It* weekly, which lists musical and free events.

To cope with the large summer influx of young people, *Use It* provides some alternative accommodation. **Sleep In** (6 Per Henrik Lings Alle, tel: 31 26 29 46) is a large hostel which is open from late June to the end of August (closed noon to 16.00hrs) and the price includes shower and locker as well as bed and breakfast. You need a sleeping bag.

Taxis
Recognisable by the green TAXA (taxi) sign on its roof and the illuminated *fri* (free) sign in the front windscreen, taxis are an expensive way to travel, but there are plenty of them in main towns. Taxis are metered and the tip is included in the price.

Telephones
Danish public telephones work efficiently both for national and international calls, but some phones do not refund your money if the call is not answered. The only solution is to insert the smallest amount of money, or to try always to make more than one call.

For internal calls, lift the receiver, put in two 25-øre coins and wait for the dialling tone; for long-distance calls, put in at least Dkr5 or 10. On newer

> **Useful dialling codes from Denmark to:**
> Australia 009 61
> Canada 009 1
> Ireland 009 353
> UK 009 44
> US 009 1
> Always follow the above with the area code (minus the initial zero), then the number. The international dialling code for Denmark from Australia is 0011 45; from Ireland 16 45; from the UK 010 45; from the US and Canada 011 45 .

telephones, dial the number first and insert coins only when the phone rings at the other end.

For more information about **long-distance** calls, tel: 114; to **reverse the charges**, tel: 115; for **general help**, tel: 140.

At Copenhagen main railway station there is a **TeleCom Centre** which provides full office facilities.

Time
Denmark is on Central European Time (GMT+1), which is one hour ahead of Britain, six hours ahead of New York, nine hours behind Sydney and 11 hours behind New Zealand.

Summer Time (GMT+2) is observed from the last Sunday in March to the last Saturday in September.

Tipping
Tipping does not exist in Denmark – the service is included in hotel and restaurant bills and in taxi fares. Hairdressers and theatre ushers do not expect tips.

DIRECTORY

Frøbjerg Hill, Funen

Toilets

Usually indicated by a pictograph, or marked WC, *toiletter*, or *Damer/Herrer*, public toilets are clean, fresh, well supplied with paper and often come with own washbasin – and they are usually free.

Tourist Offices

In Denmark, *turistinformationen* (tourist offices) are usually centrally situated and well signed from the edge of town (a white letter *i* on a green background). The staff are very helpful, well informed and speak several languages. They will book local accommodation

for visitors without charge. The offices keep a vast stack of literature, not only about their own town and area but about the rest of Denmark too. Brochures cover towns, sights and accommodation as well as nature walks, children's entertainment and local activities. Information about trains is usually available at the railway station.

The brochures are usually translated into German and English, less often into French and Italian.

LANGUAGE

Danish is a Germanic language, close to Swedish and Norwegian, and many words are similar to German. But it is a difficult language to pronounce because some letters (d, g) are silent in the middle or at the end of words, h before a v becomes silent, and some specifically Scandinavian vowels (æ,ø, å), are awkward to say correctly. But the Danes are aware of this problem and most speak very good English.

In the Danish alphabet, the following letters come after z: Æ, Ø, Å. In lists, Legoland, for example, precedes Læsø, and Århus comes at the end of the alphabet. Å is the same as AA, and should be used instead of it, but the city of Aalborg prefers to use AA.

The following words should help you to get around and read menus (which are often also in English and German).

yes ja
no nej
please vær så venlig
thank you tak
hello hej
goodbye farvel
good morning godmorgen
good afternoon goddag
good evening godaften
good night godnat

entrance indgang
no entry ingen adgang
  (for pedestrians)
exit udgang
no exit ingen udgang
emergency exit nødudgang
push/pull skub/træk or
  tryk/træk

ladies damer
gentlemen herrer
toilets toiletter
open åben
closed lukket
no smoking rygning forbudt
arrival ankomst
departure afgang
timetable køreplan
townplan bykort
step down/up trin ned /op
no standing rejs Dem ikke op

Monday mandag
Tuesday tirsdag
Wednesday onsdag
Thursday torsdag
Friday fredag
Saturday lørdag
Sunday søndag
opening times åbningstider
o'clock klokken
exhibition udstilling
petrol benzin
car bil
do not touch må ikke berøres
railway station banegård
railway line jernbane
street gade
ferry færge
no entry (cars) ingen indkørsel
Great Britain Storbritannien
USA De Forenede Stater

Food
breakfast morgenmad
lunch frokost
dinner middagsmad
starters forretter
soups supper
main courses hovedretter
fish dishes fiskeretter
cold dishes fra det kolde
  køkken
hot dishes fra det varme
  køkken
baked bagt
roast helstegt, steg
steamed dampet

smoked røget
pork flæsk, svine
chicken kylling
boiled chicken høne/hønse
white bread franskbrød
rye bread rugbrød
French bread flûte
Danish pastry Wienerbrød
butter smør
shellfish skaldyr
herring sild
trout ørred
cod torsk
shrimps rejer
vegetables grøntsager
onion løg
peas ærter

potatoes kartofler
red cabbage rødkål
carrot gulerod
cheese ost
fruit salad frugtsalat

coffee/tea kaffe/the
house wine husets vin
red/white rød/hvid
apple juice æblemost
orange juice appelsinjuice
full cream milk sødmælk
less fatty milk letmælk
skimmed milk skummetmælk

*The Tycho Brahe Planetarium,
Copenhagen*

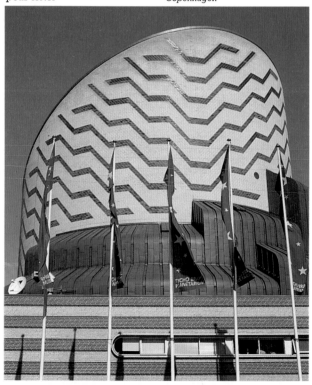

INDEX

ACKNOWLEDGEMENTS
The Automobile Asociation wishes to thank the following photographers and libraries for
their assistance in the preparation of this book.

DEREK FORSS took all the photographs and cover (AA PHOTO LIBRARY) except:

J ALLAN CASH PHOTOLIBRARY 57 Silkeborg Lakes
THE DANISH TOURIST BOARD 7 Elderly Dane (Somer), Dane (Carrebye), 11 Fanø toddler
(Nebbia), 20 Toy Museum (Crone), 42 Ærøskøbing (Pressehuset), 58 Skagen shore
(Brimberg), 71 Samsø (Sommer), 83 Kalundborg (Lennard), 89 Rebild Hills (Sommer), 117
entertainment (Johnsen)
MARY EVANS PICTURE LIBRARY 6 The Emperor's New Clothes
NATURE PHOTOGRAPHERS LTD 87 Red-backed shrike (Kevin Carlson)
JUDITH SAMSON 61 Windmill at Skagen
SPECTRUM COLOUR LIBRARY 25 the Bażarbygningen, 27 Town Hall Square, 69 Old Town
Museum
ZEFA PICTURE LIBRARY (UK) LTD 41 Langeland